I Believe in God the Father Almighty, Creator of Heaven and Earth

I Believe in God the Father Almighty, Creator of Heaven and Earth

Studies in the Theology of Creation
Volume 1

Edited by Gideon Lazar

St. Basil Institute Press

Table of Contents

Preface

The St. Basil Institute for the Study of the Theology of Creation is an institute dedicated to more deeply probing the mysteries of the Catholic faith, most especially the doctrine of creation. The doctrine of creation is absolutely vital to both Catholic theology itself as well as to the problems we face today. As Joseph Ratzinger (later Pope Benedict XVI) put it

> the question of what we do is decided by the ground of what we are. We can win the future only if we do not lose creation.[1]

Nonetheless, Ratzinger also points out that,

> Paradoxically, however, the creation account is noticeably and nearly completely absent from catechesis, preaching, and even theology. The creation narratives go unmentioned; it is asking too much to expect anyone to speak of them.[2]

Pope Francis has continued Pope Benedict's concern for the need to restore the theology of creation. In particular, in his encyclical *Laudato si'*, the Holy Father has offered important insights on how the theology of creation might overcome errors on both sides of the political spectrum with regard to the current ecological crisis.

For the last few years, the St. Basil Institute has hosted a number of conferences, both public and private to take up this call by the Church to reflect more seriously on the theology of creation. This collection of essays is some of the initial fruit of our project. Some of these essays come from our conferences, while other ones come from various students who have submitted essays to us. We hope that this volume will be the first in a long series of volumes dedicated to more deeply understanding the mysteries of the theology of creation.

This volume is divided into three parts. The first part is on the theology of creation itself. Our first essay is from Thomas Storck. In his essay, Storck calls our attention to the importance of the creation itself. There is a persistent Platonic temptation in history to ignore the role of nature itself, and another temptation to instead divinize nature. Storck shows how St. Thomas Aquinas provides a *via media* that

---

[1] Joseph Ratzinger, *'In the Beginning…' A Catholic Understanding of the Story of Creation and the Fall*, trans. Boniface Ramsey and Helen A. Saward, (Grand Rapids: William B. Eerdmans Publishing Company, 1995), 100.
[2] Ratzinger, ix.

neither divinizes nature nor ignores its importance as God's creation. The second essay is from Gideon Lazar. While God's initial creation remains, it is marred by original sin. However, many theologians today have sought to abandon the Church's teaching on original sin. Lazar looks back to St. Augustine, and ultimately the New Testament, to show the enduring importance of recognizing the reality of original sin. Our third essay is from Lance Gracy. Gracy considers the role of animals in the creation, and especially what St. Bonaventure might teach us about the animals.

The second part of this volume looks to Catholic Social Teaching. The fourth essay of this volume is by Gideon Lazar. Lazar looks back to how the Church in the past has appealed to the theology of creation to deal with the social crises of the past. He proposes that Pope Francis has called once again for a revival of Genesis in light of the ecological crisis. The fifth essay is by Vito Čapeta. Čapeta offers some important reasons that the theology of creation is vital for bioethics. He provides two case studies to show this: end of life care and cloning. The sixth essay is by Shawn and Beth Dougherty. Drawing on their own experience as local farmers, they provide a practical application of God's call to "have dominion" over the natural world. Finally, in our seventh essay, Gideon Lazar meditates upon the theology of work. How can God's own creative work be a source for our own?

The third and final part of this volume looks upwards to the Creator Himself. In the eighth essay of this volume, David Valerio draws on the Desert Fathers to show us how meditating upon the natural world can lead us to its Creator. Our ninth essay is by Lance Gracy. Gracy teaches us what St. Bonaventure has to say about the seven pillars of wisdom. Gracy draws a parallel between the meditations on nature provided by St. Bonaventure and those of J.R.R. Tolkien. The tenth and final essay, by Gideon Lazar, considers the problem of evil. If God is the creator of all things, and if everything God makes is good, how can there be evil in the world? Lazar, drawing on the Dionysian corpus and the Book of Job, argues that any evils God permits must be for the sake of a greater good.

We hope you are edified by these essays. You can find out more about the St. Basil Institute at https://stbasilinstitute.org/.

Thomas Storck, a convert to the Catholic faith, has been writing on Catholic social teaching, Catholic culture and related topics since the early 1980s. He is the author, translator or editor of eleven books and of numerous articles in periodicals, websites and collected volumes, including the editor of *The Glory of the Cosmos: a Catholic Approach to the Natural World*. His latest book is the edited volume, *Money, Markets and Morals: Catholic Perspectives on Economics and Finance* (En Route Books, 2024). Mr. Storck is a contributing editor of *New Oxford Review* and a member of the editorial board of *The Chesterton Review*. He received his undergraduate education at Kenyon College in Ohio and has an M.A. from St. John's College, Santa Fe.

Gideon Lazar received a BA in Classics and Medieval/ Byzantine Studies from the Catholic University of America. Having grown up in a Jewish family, he was baptized in 2018 and received into the Catholic Church in 2019. He is currently an MA Theology student at Sts. Cyril and Methodius Byzantine Catholic Seminary. He is the editor for the Creation Theology Fellowship and creates YouTube videos on his channel The Byzantine Scotist. He has published articles in *New Polity* magazine, *The Josias*, and *The American Postliberal*. He currently lives near Seattle with his wife and two kids.

Lance Gracy is a Doctoral Candidate and Teaching Fellow at the University of North Texas. His dissertation focuses on metaphysics and environmental philosophy in the Collationes in Hexaëmeron of St. Bonaventure. He received his M.A. in Philosophy from the University of Texas-San Antonio.

Vito Čapeta is a master's student in bioethics at Regina Apostolorum Pontifical Athenaeum. He writes for the Creation Theology Fellowship on the relationship between Catholic Social Teaching, especially on bioethical issues, and creation theology.

Shawn and Beth Dougherty have been farming together since the 1980's, for the last twenty years in eastern Ohio, where they manage their farm and 30 acres at a nearby Franciscan Convent, much of it designated by the state as 'not suitable for agriculture'. Using intensive grazing as the primary source of food energy, they raise dairy and beef cows, sheep, farm-fed hogs, and a variety of poultry, producing most of the food, feed and fertility for humans and animals, on the farm. Concerned that farming is so often dependent upon multiple off-farm resources, from feed, fuel and fertilizer to water and electricity, their ongoing project is to identify and test the means by which farming was done for centuries with a minimum of off-farm inputs. Their research has led them to identify grass conversion, especially the daily conversion of grass into milk by dairy ruminants, as a key to whole-farm sustainability, combined with the integrated nutrient feedbacks that are possible with a community of diverse animal and plant species, domestic and native.   They are the authors of *The Independent Farmstead*, Chelsea Green Press 2016.

David Valerio is a biogeochemist striving for a transfigured Creation whose professional work focuses on catalyzing nature-based solutions to the climate and biodiversity crises. He holds a BS in Geology from Texas A&M University, a MS in Earth Science from Rice University, and is working on a MA in Theology at the Byzantine Catholic Seminary of Saints Cyril and Methodius.

Part I: Historical and Speculative Studies

1

The Persistent Temptation: Man's Recurring Rejection of God's Creation

Thomas Storck

In Sacred Scripture we read of God's judgment on his new creation, that "behold, it was very good" (Genesis 1:31). And from this divine assessment of his creative works, uttered at the very beginning of the world, we can derive what should be our own attitude and valuation of creation. As something that is "very good, " what follows from our part ought to be respect and care, awe, even love. In neither authentic Hebrew nor Christian revelation do we find such statements as this one from the Buddhist tradition, that the body is like a wound, "Covered with clammy skin, with nine openings, a great wound, " which "oozes from every pore, unclean and stinking."[1] In contrast to the Second Person of the Trinity assuming a real human nature, it is said that the

> Buddha's physical body, his human and earthly life, his birth, enlightenment and death, were not really real, but a mere show conjured up to teach and awaken people.... The real Buddha should not be mistaken for the historical Buddha, who is no more than a phantom body displayed by Him [sic].[2]

This kind of attitude toward the body and the entire created world is not confined to Eastern religions, but was present in the Hellenistic world as well, for example in Gnosticism, where the "*creator god*...is placed on a lower level" than the true but unknowable supreme god. The actual creator of the world, the "Demiurge...is a secondary divine being, who, himself a proud, ambitious and impure spirit, has created this most unsatisfactory world."[3]

Thus we find that, strangely enough, this pull toward a rejection of creation or of the natural is not uncommon in the varied cultures of

---

[1] Quoted in William Theodore de Bary, ed., *The Buddhist Tradition in India, China & Japan* (New York: Vintage, 1972), pp. 35-6. In contrast are some of our Lord's miracles of healing which involved the use of his own spittle. Cf. Mark 7:33, 8:23; John 9:6. Not to mention, of course, our redemption by his Blood.

[2] Edward Conze, "Buddhism and Gnosis" in Robert A. Segal, ed., *The Allure of Gnosticism* (Chicago: Open Court, 1995), p. 177.

[3] *Ibid.*, p. 179.

mankind, sometimes accompanied by an antinomian acceptance of unrestrained bodily pleasure, for if the physical is evil or of no importance, then what does it matter how we use it? We shall see later that such an attitude is by no means dead in today's world.

But although the Jewish and Christian traditions repudiated this rejection of God's creation, this does not mean that within these cultures there were never any influences that posed a threat to God's statement that all he had created was "very good." I will deal here with what seem to me the three most important instances of this, that is, of a contest or struggle between the unambiguous acceptance of God's creative work and its Gnostic-like rejection, in whole or in part. These three instances are, first, the conflict between St. Thomas Aquinas and the older Augustinian school over Aristotle's view of nature and particularly human nature, then, the radical embrace by Descartes of a view of man that Maritain calls "angelism," and, finally, in our own time, the culmination of this potent resurgence of a Gnostic view of matter, and particularly of the body, as shown in our acceptance of homosexual activity as normative and even more so in the bizarre phenomenon of transgenderism, or better, transsexualism.

We might introduce the first of these historical junctures by quoting some words of Josef Pieper.

> In the strife between Thomas Aquinas and medieval Augustinianism two of the most revealing points in dispute were the following. Thomas taught the unity of the substantial form, while Augustinianism accepted *several* form-giving principles in man. Thomas asserted that all our knowledge, including the spiritual, and also our knowledge of God, took its starting point (and therefore always remained somehow dependent upon) sense perception, while Augustinianism claimed that spiritual knowledge was independent of sense perception. At first sight, this appears to be a petty quarrel between "schools." But for Thomas, it involved nothing less than the saving of creation as a visible reality from any attempt at reduction, devaluation, or sheer annihilation.[4]

Perhaps the best way of showing why this controversy was not a mere quibble or artificial scholastic debate will be by some words of G. K. Chesterton.

> The truth is that the historical Catholic Church began by being Platonist; by being rather too Platonist. Platonism was in that very golden Greek air that was breathed by the first great Greek theologians.... St. Augustine followed a natural mental evolution when he was a Platonist before he

---

[4] Josef Pieper, *The Silence of Saint Thomas* (Chicago: Regnery, c. 1957), p. 29.

was a Manichean, and a Manichean before he was a Christian.[5]

And Chesterton goes on to say,

> Granted all the grandeur of Augustine's contribution to Christianity, there was in a sense a more subtle danger in Augustine the Platonist than even in Augustine the Manichee. There came from it a mood which unconsciously committed the heresy of dividing the substance of the Trinity. It thought of God too exclusively as a Spirit who purifies or a Saviour who redeems; and too little as a Creator who creates. That is why men like Aquinas thought it right to correct Plato by an appeal to Aristotle; Aristotle who took things as he found them, just as Aquinas accepted things as God created them.[6]

At this point I must interrupt my argument briefly. I am not unaware that there is a tendency today to downplay Aquinas's dependence upon Aristotle and emphasize his reliance on Augustine and even on Plato and the Neo-Platonists. And insofar as this corrects an earlier one-sided view, it is all for the good. But like many corrections in intellectual history, it, in my opinion, has gone too far. Moreover, my suspicion is that this scholarly turn is not unconnected with the general Platonic atmosphere of our age. I do not have space to say anything further on this here; I simply note the existence of this controversy and my awareness of it.[7]

To return to Chesterton, then, what does he mean by saying that "the historical Catholic Church began by being Platonist; by being rather too Platonist"? We might begin to understand this by a comment that Pieper makes on Aquinas.

> Once Thomas refers to several Fathers of the Church who held that the reproduction of the human race in Paradise must have taken place in some nonsexual manner. With utter calmness, objectivity, but also absolute firmness, St. Thomas replies: *Hoc non dicitur rationabiliter*, "This cannot be said reasonably, for what belongs to the nature of man is neither taken from him nor given to him by reason of sin."[8]

---

[5] *St. Thomas Aquinas*, in *The Collected Works of G. K. Chesterton*, vol. 2, (San Francisco: Ignatius, c. 1986), p. 464

[6] *Ibid.*, p. 468.

[7] But this controversy is not altogether new, at least as regards Aristotle. As far back as the 1920s Haskins speaks of "those recent writers who minimize the differences between these two and remind us that Aristotle is at times quite Platonic." Charles Homer Haskins, *The Renaissance of the Twelfth Century* (Cleveland: World, [1927] 1957), p. 342.

[8] Josef Pieper, *Guide to Thomas Aquinas* (Notre Dame: University of Notre Dame, 1987), p. 122. Pieper is referring to *Summa Theologiae* I, q. 98, art. 2.

In such an opinion one might see a Platonism gone wild, to adopt a Chestertonian mode of expression. Nor was St. Thomas unaware of the Platonic influence on Augustine of which Chesterton spoke. On at least one occasion he rejects an opinion of that great doctor, remarking that, "This mode of speaking was usual among Platonists, with whose doctrine Augustine was imbued...."[9]

One might be surprised at the almost casual way Thomas rejects the view of more than one Father, with a simple "This cannot be said reasonably." But if we recall the matter-of-fact attitude toward sexuality evidenced by St. Paul,[10] we can see that Thomas is engaged in an act of recovering what was obscured by the Platonism that "was in that very golden Greek air that was breathed by the first great Greek theologians."

But of course this question of Platonism touches on things more fundamental than sexuality, for they go to the very root of God's creative act. As Scripture poetically says, "the Lord God formed man of dust from the ground and breathed into his nostrils the breath of life; and man became a living being" (Genesis 2:7). We were made creatures of body and soul, with not merely a vegetative or sensitive soul, as in plants and other animals, but a rational soul. However, our rational souls depend upon the knowledge received through the bodily senses, so that (as Pieper wrote) "all our knowledge, including the spiritual, and also our knowledge of God, took its starting point (and therefore always remained somehow dependent upon) sense perception." This is simply a fact, and to deny it in an attempt to make man more spiritual than God made him is to falsify what we are and to devalue the creative act of God. "To affirm and accept the reality of creation in all its provinces is the response befitting quite particularly the Christian."[11] If we err about man, about any aspect of creation, we will end up by erring about everything. And just as the Gnostic assignment of creation to an evil or secondary god could lead eventually to sexual license, so any error about creation can have unexpected consequences. As Aristotle famously remarked, "the least

---

[9] II-II, q. 23, art. 2. *Hic enim modus loquendi consuetus est apud Platonicos, quorum doctrinis imbutus fuit Augustinus; quod quidam non advertentes, ex verbis ejus sumpserunt occasionem errandi.*

[10] E.g., I Corinthians 7:1-9 or I Timothy 5:11-14.

[11] Josef Pieper, *The Silence of St. Thomas*, p. 31.

initial deviation from the truth is multiplied later a thousandfold."[12]

We have already seen that one of the important questions over which Thomas differed from the Augustinian school was the question of the soul as the form of the body. "Thomas taught the unity of the substantial form, while Augustinianism accepted *several* form-giving principles in man," wrote Pieper. What does this mean and what implications does it have?

> The human rational soul, the principle of the activity of thinking, is according to Thomas the essential form of the human body. The soul shares its own substantial being with the body, so that...a single being and life becomes the human being. There is in man a single soul, even the rational soul, which is the principle of rational, sensitive and vegetative life....[13]

Why is this point important? If the immediate connection between body and rational soul is denied, we have something which curiously resembles the earlier Gnostic relegation of material creation to a lesser god. The Gnostics feared to contaminate the purity of their highest god by contact with the material. In a similar way, the positing of a number of substantial forms in man allows for a separation between our rational souls and our bodies. It is not our rational soul that is the principle of our animal and vegetative actions, sense perception or nutrition, for example, but an other and lesser soul. God forbid that we would sully our highest and rational principle with such base acts as eating - or worse. But the recognition by Thomas of the unity of substantial form in man confers meaning on our entire earthly life. Martin Grabmann quotes Tillmann Pesch, "The upholding of this truth possesses therefore a great significance, because this places for man the worth of this world, of earthly being, in the correct light."[14]

If we make this radical separation between aspects of man which directly relate to God, and other, lesser aspects which are mediated by several layers of intervening principles, safeguards, as it were, for the higher soul, two tendencies result. One is the devaluation of many of the human things of this world. One of the theologians of the Augustinian school, what Grabmann calls the "hyperconservative circles," wrote "*Inutilis inquisitio studium philosophiae*," The study of

---

[12] *De Caelo*, bk. I, 5.

[13] Martin Grabmann, *Die Kulturphilosophie des Hl. Thomas von Aquin* (Augsburg: Benno Filser, 1925), p. 44. My translation from the German.

[14] Quoted in Grabmann, *Kulturphilosophie*, p. 51.

philosophy is a useless occupation.[15] But it is not only philosophy, but the arts, social and political life, the family, all come to be regarded as not really worthy of study or concern on the part of the believer. God is all that matters; we may forget that, after all, he did go to the trouble, so to speak, of creating something, something which he pronounced "very good." As Chesterton put it, with poetic passion,

> The really narrow Augustinians, the men who saw the Christian life only as the narrow way, the men who could not even comprehend the great Dominican's exultation in the blaze of Being, or the glory of God in all his creatures, the men who continued to insist feverishly on every text, or even every truth, that appeared pessimistic or paralysing, these gloomy Christians could not be extirpated from Christendom; and they remained and waited for their chance. The narrow Augustinians, the men who would have no science or reason or rational use of secular things, might have been defeated in controversy, but they had an accumulated passion of conviction.[16]

But we may go even further. By making our knowledge of God to some degree dependent on direct divine illumination of our intellects, as the Augustinian school tended to do, we eventually rid ourselves not just of knowledge of God, but of God himself. Thomas had insisted on the demonstrability of God's existence and of certain other matters, such as the immortality of the human soul. After his death, with the coming of the nominalists, the thought of the older Augustinian school returned in a new guise and with a decided vengeance. But now instead of our direct illumination to allow us to know God, we are gradually led to a fideism or an agnosticism or, finally, an atheism.

To jump ahead of myself a bit, we can see another example of splitting off knowledge of God from other knowledge in the modern scientific enterprise. Looking for the origins of secularism, Terence Nichols locates it

> with the separation of God from nature, a split that began in the late medieval and early modern period. This resulted in the (perceived) separation of God from everyday life that is so characteristic of contemporary secular societies. The main carrier of this has been modern natural science. Science came to understand nature as a mechanical system that operated more or less independently from God. God was thus

---

[15] Quoted in Grabmann, *Kulturphilosophie*, p. 112.

[16] Chesterton, *St. Thomas Aquinas*, pp. 546-7.

gradually (over centuries) removed from the cosmos.[17]

For our purposes here, we can note that the "separation of God from everyday life" is a result of the separation of God from man, from man's nature, from man's knowledge. For a long time a deistic God was generally considered as a necessary explanation for the complexity and order we perceive around us. Then with Darwin this was explained, or explained away, and European man easily discarded the idea of God. He had already been relegated to a separate realm; it was now easy to regard that realm as no longer necessary. To insist that we hold on to God by an act of faith made in a fideistic manner would not work outside the kinds of isolated cultural milieux characteristic of certain types of American Protestantism. Such an approach could survive hostile attacks only by its isolation, and in the long run could not even withstand the reasoned criticisms generated from within its own sphere.

It is difficult to exaggerate the significance of the work of St. Thomas on this matter. Both Chesterton and Pieper point out the fact that the intellectual and spiritual trajectory within Latin Christendom required a rethinking of these matters. To separate the rational soul from the body by a series of intermediate substantial forms might seem like a harmless philosophical or theological construct, but it can end up with the body as an extra, a prison for the soul, useless baggage, even as the enemy of the soul conceived as the only real and true human being. The logical outcome of such views we will see when we look at events closer to our own time.

But, of course, all this, however important, is not the fundamental point. For as Pieper wrote, "It would be understating the case to assert that Thomas `defends' natural reality; to his mind it would be utterly ridiculous for man to undertake to defend the creation. Creation needs no justification."[18] It is a question of truth. The view of human nature contained in the New Testament is that of a unity of soul and body, in fact, of the resurrection of our bodies. Thomas follows this truth logically when he affirms that "The soul united with the body is more like God than the soul separated from the body because it (the soul in the body) possesses its nature in more complete fashion."[19] G. K.

---

[17] Terence L. Nichols, *The Sacred Cosmos: Christian Faith and the Challenge of Naturalism.* (Grand Rapids: Brazos Press, c. 2003), p. 9.

[18] *Guide to Thomas Aquinas*, pp. 121-22

[19] Quoted in Pieper, *Guide to Thomas Aquinas*, p. 122.

Chesterton once again,

> Now nobody will begin to understand the Thomist philosophy, or indeed the Catholic philosophy, who does not realize that the primary and fundamental part of it is entirely the praise of Life, the praise of Being, the praise of God as the Creator of the World. Everything else follows a long way after that, being conditioned by various complications like the Fall or the vocation of heroes.[20]

Thomas was simply restoring truths obscured over the course of several centuries. Truths that are of vital importance, but that again and again are forgotten or downplayed, often in the interests of having what seems a more spiritual, and hence better, outlook. We must never forget, though, that spiritual does not necessary equate with good. Satan and his fallen angels are purely spiritual creatures. We are not such, and to pretend that we are is not only false but opens the way for colossal errors and evils, as we will see shortly. As Chesterton said, speaking of those theologians whose views Thomas corrected, "they were less orthodox in being more spiritual."[21]

Thomas won this battle. Despite the fierce attacks on his teaching made after his death, he was vindicated by the Church at his canonization in 1323. But there is a strange tug in human nature, a tendency to over and over again deny an essential part of itself, namely the bodily. We are so accustomed to thinking of the bodily appetites as occasions of sin - as indeed they often are - that we can fail to recognize this chronic tendency for what it really is, a refusal to accept God's creation in its fullness. This St. Thomas would never accept. But modernity not only accepted this heresy but has again and again embraced it with enthusiasm. Let us now look at one of the most notable instances of this.

With the coming of modernity we see numerous signs of changes in our intellectual and cultural outlooks, but there is one that is especially important for us today. This is the elaboration of the new philosophical system by the Frenchman, René Descartes. Although as we just saw, mankind has been tempted again and again to reject nature, in whole or in part, with Descartes we witness the creation of a philosophical system with, one might say, that aim specifically in mind, and a system that continues to have immense influence on the world.

---

[20] *St. Thomas Aquinas*, pp. 483-4.

[21] *St. Thomas Aquinas*, p. 434.

There are created beings we call angels. As Jacques Maritain put it, "*thinking substances* in the true sense of the word, pure subsistent forms,... but they do not inform matter and are free from the vicissitudes of time, movement, generation and corruption...."[22] But we are not such. As we saw before, our knowledge even of purely spiritual things depends, according to St. Thomas, in the first instance on our sense knowledge. To endeavor to reshape man as a purely spiritual creature becomes what Maritain calls the "sin of *angelism*."[23] On Descartes's view, however,

> the human soul is not only subsistent as the ancients taught, causing the body to exist with its own existence; it has, without the body, received direct from God all the operative perfection which can befit it. There is the destruction of the very reason of its union with the body.... For if the body and the senses are not the necessary means of the acquisition of its ideas for that soul, and consequently the instrument by which it rises to its own perfection, which is the life of the intelligence and the contemplation of truth, then,...the body and senses can be there for nothing but to provide the soul - which needs only itself and God in order to think, - with means for the practical subjugation of the earth and all material nature, and this reduces the soul's good to the domination of the physical universe.[24]

We already saw that the medieval Augustinian tradition posited a number of successive forms in man, separating the rational soul from immediate contact with the body. But in Descartes the body becomes something really extraneous, inexplicable.

> His dualism, in particular - which makes man...a complete spiritual substance...joined in an absolutely unintelligible manner to an extended substance which is also complete and exists and lives without the soul - is only the translation into the order of Being of a doctrine which, in the order of knowledge, attributes to the human soul the functions of the pure spirit.[25]

If the human soul knows according to the angelic manner, then the body is indeed "for the practical subjugation of the earth and all material nature, and this reduces the soul's good to the domination of the physical universe."

---

22 Jacques Maritain, *Three Reformers: Luther, Descartes, Rousseau* (London: Sheed & Ward, 1947), p. 55.

23 Maritain, *Three Reformers*, p. 54.

24 Maritain, *Three Reformers*, pp. 63-4.

25 Maritain, *Three Reformers*, p. 83.

Discovering himself with a body, however much that might be inconvenient for his new-found philosophy, and coming to believe that that body and its senses have nothing to do with intellectual knowledge, what does one do with that body? Well, as European man was just beginning to see at that time, there was quite a bit one could do with it, indeed, a brilliant career, as it were, was opening up for the body in the control of nature. Descartes himself is quite clear about his desire to turn philosophy into just such a tool for technological exploitation. He wrote that he wanted

> instead of that speculative philosophy which is taught in the Schools, we may find a practical philosophy by means of which...we can...render ourselves the masters and possessors of nature.[26]

But a tool was needed to translate this aspiration into practical results, and the tool which was found to be so potent for this purpose was mathematics, the mathematical understanding of nature, in which whatever could not be treated mathematically was in practice disregarded or ignored. This importation into philosophy of a mathematical method was indeed an essential part of Descartes' approach.

> The philosophy of Descartes may be said to be a universal mathematics. His philosophical method, from which his entire system comes, is the method of mathematics.... The special method of mathematics in philosophical generalizations is the comprehensive and original strength of his philosophical system, the source of its deepest epistemological foundations.[27]

Nor was this place for mathematics something unique to Descartes. In the insightful introduction to his 1954 work, *English Literature in the Sixteenth Century*, C. S. Lewis wrote of the scientific revolution of early modern Europe:

> What was fruitful in the thought of the new scientists was the bold use of mathematics in the construction of hypotheses, tested not by observation simply but by controlled observation of phenomena that could be precisely measured. On the practical side it was this that delivered Nature into our hands. And on our thoughts and emotions...it was destined to have profound effects. By reducing Nature to her mathematical elements it substituted a mechanical for a genial or animistic conception of the universe. The world was emptied, first of her

---

[26] *Discourse on Method*, Part VI.

[27] Fritz R. Kühn, *Descartes' Verhältnis zur Mathematik und Physik* (Munich: Rösl, 1923), p. 33. My translation from the German.

> indwelling spirits, then of her occult sympathies and antipathies, finally of her colours, smells, and tastes.... The result was dualism rather than materialism. The mind, on whose ideal constructions the whole method depended, stood over against its object in ever sharper dissimilarity. Man, with his new powers became rich like Midas but all that he touched had gone dead and cold. This process, slowly working, ensured during the next century the loss of the old mythical imagination: the conceit, and later the personified abstraction, takes its place. Later still, as a desperate attempt to bridge a gulf which begins to be found intolerable, we have the Nature poetry of the Romantics.[28]

There are at least two important points to note in this passage. In the first place, Lewis explains how the mathematical treatment of the natural world worked. Only what was measurable was real because only what was measurable could be manipulated; hence "colours, smells, and tastes" were banished. Nature was reduced to a colorless, lifeless world, and later to a mass of electrons moving about rapidly in a void. Sir Arthur Eddington's famous description of his "two tables" illustrates this memorably.

> I have settled down to the task of writing these lectures and have drawn up my chairs to my two tables....
>
> One of them has been familiar to me from earliest years. It is a commonplace object of that environment which I call the world.... It has extension; it is comparatively permanent; it is coloured; above all it is *substantial*.... It is a *thing*...
>
> Table No. 2 is my scientific table.... It does not belong to the world previously mentioned - that world which spontaneously appears around me when I open my eyes... My scientific table is mostly emptiness. Sparsely scattered in that emptiness are numerous electric charges rushing about with great speed; but their combined bulk amounts to less than a billionth of the bulk of the table itself.... I need not tell you that modern physics has by delicate test and remorseless logic assured me that my second scientific table is the only one which is really there....[29]

But there is more: "The mind," Lewis wrote, "on whose ideal constructions the whole method depended, stood over against its object in ever sharper dissimilarity." The objects of the mind's "constructions," however, were not merely things like tables. With Descartes it is already clear that one of those objects was the human

---

[28] *English Literature in the Sixteenth Century* (Oxford: University of Oxford, 1954), pp. 3-4.

[29] *The Nature of the Physical World*, (New York: Macmillan, 1929), pp. ix-x, xii.

body itself. And in time, not just the body but the human mind, the very human person. But we will save this consideration for later.

In the midst of this mathematical orientation of thought the European mind rested in admiration for some time, as in Alexander Pope's encomium to Newton (in a projected epitaph), and thus to the entire mathematical reconstruction of nature.

Nature and Nature's Laws lay hid in Night

God said, Let Newton be, and All was Light.

This did not and could not last, but instead it created, as Lewis noted, "a gulf which begins to be found intolerable." Thus the Romantic reaction against the cold universalism of the age of Descartes.

This reaction took varied and even contradictory forms. Currents of thought mutated in peculiar ways; the same idea could give rise to reactions at odds with one another. I think we can sum up the Romantic recoil against the new science and philosophy under six headings. These are the intellectual or aesthetic movements toward the particular, toward anti-rationalism, toward a rejection of any form of Christianity, toward medievalism, toward the strange and preternatural and even the diabolic, finally toward Thomism. These did not occur one after the other, however, for most of them were happening simultaneously. Let us briefly look at each one of these.

For Descartes, and for the thinkers of the Enlightenment, nature was something of interest as *types*, as abstractions even, not as individual things which could be seen and touched. This was true even of thinkers not wholly within the mainstream of Enlightenment thought, such as Samuel Johnson. In his novel, *Rasselas*, the poet Imlac explains to Rasselas that "The business of a poet is to examine, not the individual, but the species; to remark general properties, and large appearances; he does not number the streaks of the tulip, or describe the different shades in the verdure of the forest."[30] This in contrast with the poetry of Wordsworth, Coleridge or Keats, who "described natural phenomena" with so much "accuracy of observation,"[31] which is a way of describing nature that has come to be taken for granted. But one notes that it is only with the universal that rational thought can exist. Concern with only the particular, which

---

[30] *Rasselas, Prince of Abyssinia* (New York: Robert Carter, 1855 [1759]), p. 47.

[31] "Introduction: The Romantic Period," *The Norton Anthology of English Literature* (New York: W. W. Norton, rev. ed., c. 1968), vol. 2, p. 9.

can be a form of nominalism, will destroy philosophy. As a modern Thomist put it, "no demonstrative knowledge deals with a singular thing as singular."[32]

As a result, this turn to the individual and particular could easily go hand-in-hand with an anti-rational strain of thinking and lead to a denial of the value of scholastic thinking. Among Catholics it was present in thinkers who downplayed or denied the role of reason in theology, such as the French priest, Louis Bautain (d. 1867), who was required by Pope Gregory XVI to affirm the ability of human reason to prove the existence of God, or Louis Bonald (d. 1846) and Augustin Bonnetty (d. 1879), who had located the foundations of theology not in the mind's rational apprehension of the preambles of Faith but in a supposed tradition handed down from a primitive revelation.

Just as today, moreover, in some minds a reaction against the Cartesian rejection of nature became chiefly a reaction against Christianity, as they understood it, chiefly against Protestant Christianity, which did and does include a tendency to narrow reality down to simply God and the soul. This was already leading in the nineteenth century to a longing for a vanished paganism, or even to an attempt to revive it. We can see this as early as 1866 in the English poet, Algernon Charles Swinburne's poem, "Hymn to Proserpine," containing the famous line (part of which is said to have been the dying words of the Emperor Julian the Apostate), "Thou hast conquered, O pale Galilean; the world has grown gray from thy breath...." And the bodily, and even erotic, note is explicitly struck:

> Wilt thou yet take all, Galilean? But these thou shalt not take -
>
> The laurel, the palms, and the paean, the breasts of the nymphs in the brake,
>
> Breasts more soft than a dove's, that tremble with tenderer breath;
>
> And all the wings of the Loves, and all the joy before death....

But Swinburne was profoundly mistaken. It was not authentic Christianity that devalued the body, it was a movement that arose in opposition to the central voice, the central path, of Christian thought, which was that of St. Thomas. Speaking of Aquinas' affirmation that man is not merely a soul, Chesterton says that "this is in some ways a naturalistic notion, very near to the modern respect for material things;

---

[32] George P. Klubertanz, *Introduction to the Philosophy of Being* (New York: Appleton-Century-Crofts, c. 1955), p. 14.

a praise of the body that might be sung by Walt Whitman or justified by D. H. Lawrence...."[33] And he is right, as far as that goes. For whatever truths were confusedly seen by Walt Whitman or D. H. Lawrence or Swinburne are, like all truths, Christian truths because they are natural truths, and they find their proper setting within the whole corpus of Christian doctrine, of the Christian account of the world, of reality, of ourselves as creatures of body and soul. As we will see, when they are taken out of this context, they easily turn upon themselves and contradict what was previously seen as their central affirmation.

Finally, the remaining notes of Romanticism that I mentioned: medievalism, the hankering after the strange and preternatural, Thomism. The nostalgia for a lost world before modern science and philosophy had endowed man with "new powers" with which he became "rich like Midas but all that he touched [became] dead and cold" manifested itself in varying and conflicting ways. But if we want to go back beyond the scientific revolution then it is the Middle Ages that we encounter. Interest in the collection of old ballads and fairy tales, something that began during the eighteenth century itself, the new genre of Gothic romances which began as early as 1764 with Horace Walpole's *Castle of Otranto*, the frank longing for the lost Catholic unity of Europe as in Novalis' *Die Christenheit oder Europa* of 1799 - all these and more were signs of such a medievalism. It served as the backdrop for many a literary work, novels of Walter Scott, Keat's poem, "The Eve of St. Agnes," and many others. In architecture it led to the Gothic revival and many fine buildings, and was in part responsible for the Oxford Movement in the Anglican Communion. And it did lead many sincere souls into the Catholic Church.

An interest in the old and far-away not unnaturally led to an interest in the strange and preternatural. Coleridge's fine 1798 poem, "The Rime of the Ancient Mariner," with its commentary taken in part from the medieval Byzantine scholar, Michael Psellus' speculations on various spiritual creatures, "the invisible inhabitants of this planet, neither departed souls nor angels.... They are very numerous and there is no climate or element without one or more"[34] is an outstanding example. The German writer of fantastic and gruesome fiction, E. T.

---

[33] Chesterton, *St. Thomas Aquinas*, p. 434.

[34] See Coleridge's commentary at the end of Part II of the poem.

A. Hoffmann (d. 1822), was an influence on Edgar Allan Poe, whose work in turn influenced Baudelaire, who translated him into French, all of which illustrates the complex aesthetic and intellectual genealogy of the century.

But an interest in the macabre also led to an interest in drugs and altered states of consciousness, which we see as early as Coleridge himself and Thomas DeQuincey at the beginning of the century. Eventually this went to farther and darker realms, which with Joris-Karl Huysmans (d. 1907), for example, took the form of an explicit diabolism, until the author's happy return to the Church.

But within the Church there was a more solid and important medievalism, the rediscovery, if you will, of the thought of St. Thomas Aquinas. This began early in the century and the labors of these early pioneers were crowned by Leo XIII's 1878 encyclical *Aeterni Patris*. Beginning with this, and during the next eighty or so years, Catholics rallied to Thomism, and as a result we had the remarkable writings of Chesterton, Pieper, Grabmann, Maritain, Etienne Gilson, and many, many others. Thomism seemed securely seated upon the throne of Catholic intellectual life. If we can say that beginning in the nineteenth century there was a turn away from the hyper-rationalism of the previous century, and if outside of the Catholic world this reaction took the most strange and contradictory forms, it initiated within the Church a new golden age of Thomism.

But however much this focus on the thought of Aquinas was a great grace for the Church, I would be guilty of neglect if I did not mention what have been perceived as weaknesses in this movement of revival. For example, the Jesuit Frederick Copleston, in his monumental *History of Philosophy*, wrote that

> But one can hardly shut one's eyes to the fact that in many ecclesiastical institutions Thomism, or what was considered such, came to be taught in a dogmatic manner analogous to that in which Marxism-Leninism is taught in Communist dominated education.[35]

One can easily find such sentiments repeated elsewhere, and it would be foolish to deny that they had some truth. However much the teaching and study of St. Thomas was an exercise in authentic philosophy, this negative attitude certainly led to a diminished interest in Aquinas by many Catholics. But as I suggested above, I think this

---

[35] *A History of Philosophy*, (Garden City, N.Y.: Image, 1977), vol. 9, pt. 2, p. 44.

may well be part of the cultural change back to a more Platonic stance which occurred in the larger society. To quote Fr. Copleston again,

> Given the changed situation, it is arguable that the impetus of the Thomist revival is spent. With diminished official backing and with the development of tendencies in theology which are hostile to the use of metaphysics for apologetic purposes, if not to metaphysics as such, it is natural that there should be a marked reaction against Thomism.[36]

But whatever the reasons for the changed situation, this era of a renewed Thomism did not last, and so we find ourselves now in another cultural epoch, whose contours I will try to trace out.

If it is true that different historical periods are characterized by a more Platonic or a more Aristotelian cultural orientation, and that frequently one age will react against the philosophy of the previous one, what can we say about our own time? We saw in the nineteenth century a reaction against the earlier Cartesian orientation in a variety of currents of thought and sentiment in the secular world, as well as a healthy manifestation in the enthusiastic promotion of the thought of St. Thomas by Pope Leo XIII. But we are now far from that, and the decade of the 1960s seems to me the ironic turning point.

At first sight the 1960s seem to be a clear and loud endorsement of the natural, and especially of the body and all its works. Sexuality was certainly celebrated and rationality was downplayed or decried, including a recrudescence of interest in drug taking and altered states of consciousness that had characterized certain nineteenth-century thinkers. But here we can discern something interesting about this question of acceptance of the body and of sexuality as goods. When such an acceptance is divorced from its proper context, that is, from an entire philosophy of the human person, not only do they lead to sin, but they begin to contradict and in time to destroy themselves. In the 1960s sexuality was celebrated not because very many young people came to an understanding that the Cartesian mentality had distorted Western thought or, still less, because St. Thomas was being accepted as a sure guide to life. However much a vague anti-Cartesian sentiment was in the air, for most people sexuality was affirmed because it felt good. But feeling good is not a sufficient guide to life. And if heterosexuals are justified in engaging in sex simply because it feels good, with no reference whatsoever to the reason such a thing as sex even exists, then how can others, whose sexual proclivities are

---

[36] *A History of Philosophy*, vol. 9, pt. 2, p. 46.

radically against nature, be denied the same pleasures? Thus even before the decade was over the same-sex attracted were raising their voices and claiming the same rights to express their sexuality as freely as any others.

And what happened? Although until about the 1990s the movement for acceptance of homosexuality as normative did not make much headway, there was never much doubt of its ultimate success. The opposition, such as it was, centered on an Evangelical Protestant employment of biblical texts, something utterly inadequate in the context of policy debates at the end of the twentieth century. Rarely was there a voice raised to point out the obvious fact that the natural use of human sexuality, as shown in both the external and internal structure of our bodies, is oriented toward the union of the male and the female and the fruit of that union. Accordingly the protest of the 1960s in favor of a frank acceptance of the natural now became a protest in favor of doing whatever one feels like doing. What is *natural* was understood by most people as simply what I have a spontaneous inclination to do. There was no recognition that human nature was not about the individual but about the species as a whole. Nature indicates not who I am, but what I am.

But I think we can discern more. Although the nineteenth-century reaction against the Cartesian view of nature was genuine, it took, as we saw, many varied and conflicting forms. Without a firm intellectual framework it necessarily was a superficial, even emotional reaction. It lacked the substance necessary to withstand not only contrary intellectual currents but weaknesses in fallen human nature itself. So even if the nineteenth and the first half of the twentieth centuries can be said to be an age in which something like an Aristotelian approach to the natural was dominant, this does not mean that such an approach was firmly in place. Contraception, for example, became widely accepted by Protestant religious bodies before the midpoint of the century. And contraceptive use, although not as spectacular an instance of the violation of the nature of sexuality as is same-sex activity, is equally an affront to nature. So that the 1960s' longing for the natural was compromised from the outset. Indeed, it could not have flourished without easy availability of contraceptives and eventually even of abortion. In the early 60s there was an advertisement for the chemical industry with the slogan, Better Living Through Chemistry. With a supreme irony, however, very many of those who recognized the deleterious effects of the chemical industry on the natural environment turned right around and availed themselves of the products of that same industry to frustrate the natural results of their sexual activity.

Interestingly enough there was at least one voice at the time which was raised in protest and in a explicit call for a return to Aristotle. This was the American philosopher, Henry Veatch, who recognized exactly what was going on and who wrote in 1974 the following perceptive remarks.

> For is it not a singular coincidence that in the confusion worse confounded of what we might call our contemporary youth culture, any number of young people today have begun to insist that they are "turned off" by the entire range of modern science and technology? Not only that, but they would not hesitate to throw out, along with science, the whole philosophical and cultural superstructure that has been erected over our increasingly frenzied and uncritical cults of science and technology as they have been developing over the last three hundred years. Now the irony is that the very rise of so-called modern science and modern philosophy was originally associated - certainly in the minds of men like Galileo and Descartes - with a determined repudiation of Aristotle: it was precisely his influence which it was thought necessary to destroy, root and branch, before what we now know as science and philosophy in the modern mode could get off the ground. Accordingly, could it be that as so many of us today are turning our backs so bitterly on all the heretofore boasted achievements of modern culture, we might find ourselves inclined, perhaps even compelled, to return to the Aristotelianism that both antedated and was considered antithetical to the whole modern experiment in knowledge and living?[37]

By the time Professor Veatch wrote this the impetus of the counterculture was already mostly spent, lost in a mixture of bourgeois hedonism and corporate advertising, for capitalists very soon discovered that the frank sexuality of the 1960s was a potent means for moneymaking. We did not return to the Aristotelianism that Descartes and like-minded thinkers were so opposed to. Instead we repudiated what little was genuine about the counterculture's protest and by now we have gone well beyond the emerging contradictions of the late 1960s. We have a more obvious and more direct attack on the integrity of human nature and the human body. I refer, of course, to the phenomenon of transgenderism or transsexualism. With this we

---

[37] Henry Veatch, *Aristotle, a Contemporary Appreciation* (Bloomington: Indiana University, c. 1974) p. 4.

have a clear prioritizing of the mind over the body, the body reduced to a mere slave of our mental desires, the very opposite of what the 1960s claimed it was looking for. This phenomenon is a witness to the essential superficiality of the movement toward the natural and its lack of a substantial intellectual foundation, since many of those who loudly call for protection of the environment seem oddly blind to the need to protect our most intimate environment, our bodies, indeed, our very existence as a harmonious composite of body and soul. Thomas Aquinas would no doubt tell these people, No, we are not disembodied souls who happen to inhabit a body whose contours and shape are malleable according to our whims. The body tells us something definite about what we are. It cannot be ignored any more than the soul can. It is not without reason that we are called rational animals, and to forget or ignore or downplay either of those terms is to begin to destroy humanity.

As recently as the turn of the millennium it was still clear to even some secular thinkers that random mutilation of the body was probable evidence of some kind of mental disorder.[38] But when this desire to alter the body becomes linked with sex all bets are off. Now we believe ourselves to be in the realm of human liberation. Even in 1998 Jamison "James" Green could write,

> [Transgenderism] is not a fad, not a flash-in-the-pan phenomenon, but representative of a genuine cultural transition that I believe is evolving in our midst. We are trying to get our collective hands around the concepts of sex and gender, one of the last (as far as we know now) psychological and social frontiers, and if we can grasp it, understand it, and learn to live with it, I believe we can ultimately be freed from the yoke of sex and gender oppression.[39]

Although it would be too long a digression to go into this in detail here, this desire to reach and transgress any and all frontiers, psychological and social and otherwise, is simply the latest manifestation of that civilizational liberalism that began by destroying the medieval economic order with its restraints on our acquisitive appetites, and over the centuries has destroyed one pillar after another of a Christian social order, progressing from the economic and

---

[38] Carl Elliott, "A New Way to Be Mad," *The Atlantic Monthly*, December 2000, pp. 73-84.

[39] "Transgender: From the Personal to the Political" [book review], *Feminist Collections*, vol. 19, no. 2, winter 1998, pp. 14-16, quotation on p. 16.

political to the family and finally to the most intimate aspects of human life and personhood.

It is actually no surprise that we have begun treating our own bodies as simply matter for manipulation. Henri de Lubac wrote, "But, since man, too, had become an object of science like all the rest, why would what was true for the external world be any less true for man himself?"[40] If we are busy exploiting the rest of the world according to our own desires, why stop with that? Even in the midst of the Romantic reaction against Cartesianism this dream to remake all of nature lived on, even if somewhat muted, in thinkers such as Fourier or Saint-Simon. Pope Francis wrote of this seemingly ineradicable tendency in his 2015 encyclical *Laudato Si'*.

> [H]umanity has taken up technology and its development *according to an undifferentiated and one-dimensional paradigm.* This paradigm exalts the concept of a subject who, using logical and rational procedures, progressively approaches and gains control over an external object. This subject makes every effort to establish the scientific and experimental method, which in itself is already a technique of possession, mastery, and transformation.... (no. 106)

But now we ourselves are the subject. We pretend to ourselves that this will always be protected by the subject's free and informed consent. But already in our treatment of confused young people who indicate any dissatisfaction with their own sex or bodily form we have approached the limits of consent and even crossed beyond them. For why not? If something is not always forbidden because it is intrinsically wrong, then, given the right circumstances it can become a matter of persuasion or even force. For, as Pope Francis further pointed out, this attitude toward technological exploitation has affected even how we think. He notes the "tendency...to make the method and aims of science and technology an epistemological paradigm..." (no. 107). We easily usher troubled young people into a gulag of medical experimentation because we ourselves know no other way of dealing with such matters. Just as we see no need to warn consumers of the dangers of genetically modified food, we see no need to warn of the dangers of a body modified by chemicals and surgery. We know no other way of thinking or perceiving reality. And of course, there are those for whom this kind of thinking begets gigantic profits. Pope Francis once more:

---

[40] *The Drama of Atheist Humanism* (San Francisco: Ignatius, 1995 [1949]), p. 406.

We have to accept that technological products are not neutral, for they create a framework which ends up conditioning lifestyles and shaping social possibilities along the lines dictated by the interests of certain powerful groups.

> Decisions which may seem purely instrumental are in reality decisions about the kind of society we want to build. (no. 107)

If we look upon the current scene without attending to the deeper and underlying causes for what is happening, we will probably view each example of an attack on the natural order as isolated and even unique. Some will deplore the degradation of the environment, others the transgender movement. But if we can understand the past cultural and intellectual trajectory of our civilization we will see that these are not isolated events. We either accept God's creation in its entirety or we reject whatever parts of it currently displease us or which offend against contemporary fashions in thinking and feeling. We cannot pick and choose here. We must either accept God's pronouncement on his work of creation that "behold, it was very good," or we are open to altering, manipulating and destroying everything, ourselves included. That is the unavoidable choice which is ours.

2

Analyzing Augustine's Doctrine of Original Sin: A Response to John Romanides and John Meyendorff

Gideon Lazar

Original sin is today often seen as one of the dividing doctrines of the Eastern Orthodox and Catholic Churches. According to the popular story, Augustine was influenced by Neoplatonism and a mistranslation of Romans 5:12, causing him to formulate a view of original sin in which infants are personally guilty of the sin of Adam and are condemned to hell unless baptized. There is no free will and only grace can save someone. The Eastern Fathers supposedly held to a totally different view, emphasizing human free will and that only death comes through Adam. This story was most famously articulated by Eastern Orthodox theologians Fr. John Romanides and Fr. John Meyendorff. However, on a closer analysis, the story turns out to be much more complicated. Augustine carefully distinguishes different forms of sin, and the Eastern Fathers held that all mankind was present in Adam.

This essay will analyze the claims of Romanides and Meyendorff, and compare them to the historical, Augustinian, biblical, and patristic evidence. Section I will closely look at what the arguments of Romanides and Meyendorff are. Section II will analyze the history of the Pelagian controversy and look at which side was actually influenced by Neoplatonism and the reception of Pelagianism in the East. Section III will analyze what Augustine's views on original sin actually are. Section IV will analyze the various possible interpretations of the ambiguous Greek grammar of Romans 5:12. Section V will look at the Jewish context of Paul to seek further clarification on the correct interpretation of Romans. Section VI will compare Augustine to the other fathers. Section VII will then conclude by summarizing all the evidence and seeing if Romanides and Meyendorff's claims hold up to scrutiny.

I. The Theology of Romanides and Meyendorff

Romanides and Meyendorff contrast their understanding of

Augustine's view of original sin with the wider patristic consensus. Romanides lays out his views in *The Ancestral Sin*. For Romanides, the fall begins not with the fall of Adam, but with the fall of Satan.[1] It is through Satan's sin that death is introduced into the world.[2] He uses Justin Martyr and Athenagoras' discussions of the creation of the Nephilim through the sexual relations between demons and human women to prove this, although he understand these passages in these Fathers to instead refer to the "perpetuat[ion of] the fall among men after Adam." In fact, in one spot, Romanides seems to deny that the fall of man "did not happen automatically with the first-made humans." He instead says that with Adam entered into "spiritual death."[3] He claims that it only with the murder of Abel that death entered the world. In fact, he denies that any person dies because of Adam's sin, but instead insists that everyone dies because of their own sin.[4]

Elsewhere however, Romanides contradicts this model. He claims at one point that man was made "neither mortal nor or immortal" and that they would have matured into immorality but instead cut themselves off from grace.[5] It is not entirely clear how to reconcile the variety of different statements about the origins of sin and death by Romanides. Nowhere does Romanides lay out a clear point by point statement about his own view. Rather, he focuses on critiquing the positions of Augustine.

Augustine, Romanides claims, has no understanding of the role that Satan and death have in the redemption.[6] Instead, Augustine supposedly thinks that "Satan and death were nothing more than instruments in the divine wrath." Augustine is also wrong because of his belief that man is naturally immortal.[7] Romanides additionally claims that Augustine held that "the entire human race shares in Adam's guilt" because of "the justice of God." He claims that Augustine thought the human will of Adam, which was guilty of the

---

[1] Ioannes Romanides, *The Ancestral Sin: A Comparative Study of the Sin of Our Ancestors Adam and Eve According to the Paradigms and Doctrines of the First- and Second-Century Church and the Augustinian Formulation of Original Sin*, trans. George S. Gabriel, (Ridgewood: Zephyr Publishing, 2008), 69-70.

[2] Romanides, 79.

[3] Romanides, 80.

[4] Romanides, 164-68.

[5] Romanides, 158-61.

[6] Romanides, 70.

[7] Romanides, 155-56.

sin, was transferred to later descendants, and this is why they are condemned.

Romanides takes Romans 5:12 to be translated as "because of which [death] all have sinned."[8] Adam's sin causes separation from God's grace and death which causes people to fall into sin, but it does not cause others to be guilty of sin. Death causes sin because, according to Irenaeus, it is connected with corruptibility which causes weakness. Romanides takes both "in Adam all have sinned" and "because all have sinned" to both be heretical. He thinks that the meaning is obviously not this, because then the Gnostics would have used it to support the belief in the preexistence of souls. While it is clear how the latter interpretation could be held in a Gnostic sense, it is unclear how the former, which is the one Augustine held, could since the Gnostics held the preexistence and fall of all souls, not just that of Adam.

Meyendorff lays out a similar, but somewhat different, account in *Byzantine Theology: Historical Trends & Doctrinal Themes*. Meyendorff holds that the Eastern fathers say that sin can only be incurred as the result of a personal mind.[9] He claims that this is the result of Maximus' theology of the will. The "natural will" is always good and oriented towards God. It is only the personal will, the "gnomic will" which can sin. According to Photius, it would be a heresy to talk of a "sin of nature." Instead, Meyendorff sees only corruptibility and mortality as coming from Adam's sin, not "inherited guilt".[10] This also means that infants are not baptized for the remission of sins, but only to give them "a new and immortal life, which their mortal parents are unable to communicate to them."[11] He does not clarify where infants go if they die though.

Meyendorff contrasts this with Augustine, who he claims believed in inherited guilt even for infants.[12] He thinks the key verse which led to Augustine's interpretation is Romans 5:12. Augustine's error supposedly comes his use of the Latin rather than the Greek, which says "*in quo omnes peccaverunt* ('in whom all have sinned.')" The specific issue Meyendorff notes is the rendering of the Greek ἐπί as *in*.

---

[8] Romanides, 166.

[9] John Meyendorff, *Byzantine Theology: Historical Trends and Doctrinal Themes*, (New York: Fordham University Press, 1987), 143.

[10] Meyendorff, 145.

[11] Meyendorff, 145-46.

[12] Meyendorff, 144-45.

Meyendorff instead offers two translations. His first is "because all men have sinned." While Meyendorff thinks that this interpretation is possible, and he takes this as a scholarly consensus,[13] this is the very sense which Romanides condemns as Gnostic. Meyendorff does offer a second translation though, which is "because of death, all men have sinned," the same translation Romanides offers.[14] He has three main arguments for this interpretation. First, if the ᾧ is taken as masculine, it can refer back to the "immediately preceding substantive, *thanatos*." Second, it is the interpretation of the Greek Fathers. Third, it makes a connection between Romans 5:12 and 1 Corinthians 15:22 which connects the death in Adam with the rising again in Christ.

II. The Pelagian Controversy

Before looking at if Romanides or Meyendorff are correct about Augustine, it is important to look at the context in which Augustine developed his teachings on original sin. This context is the Pelagian controversy.

Pelagius was a British lay theologian from the early fifth century.[15] He spent most of his life in Rome, although fled in 410 to avoid its sack. Pelagius argued for a high degree of free will. The writings of him and his students argued that there is no original sin.[16] He even went so far as to argue that everyone has the natural ability to be moral, even apart from God's grace, although God's grace could help one be virtuous. Salvation ultimately was up to the person themselves though, not God.

Pelagius' views were highly influenced by Neoplatonism.[17] The initial popularity of Pelagianism was in part be due to the influence of Origenism, which was itself very Neoplatonic.[18] Plotinus and Porphyry emphasized how one becomes divinized through virtuous action.[19] Everyone is a part of the divine Intellect, and so they have the power within themselves to return to the divine through virtuous

---

[13] Meyendorff in particular cites Joseph Fitzgerald. Meyendorff, 149. Fitzgerald's own analysis will be taken up in section V.

[14] Meyendorff, 144.

[15] Lindsey Anne Scholl, "The Pelagian Controversy: A Heresy in its Intellectual Context," PhD diss., (University of California, Santa Barbara, 2011), 1-2.

[16] Scholl, 3.

[17] Scholl, 24-57.

[18] Scholl, 99-105.

[19] Scholl, 24-57.

action. Pelagius himself adopts this model, although he Christianizes it by removing a literal notion of humans being parts of the divine.

After Pelagius and his student, Caelestius, left Rome for North Africa, they came into contact with Augustine.[20] Augustine felt that what he was hearing from Pelagius and Caelestius about grace was heretical. While Pelagius left Africa and moved to Palestine, Caelestius remained and tried to be ordained a priest. However, a deacon objected to his ordination to the bishop and submitted a list of heresies of which Caelestius was guilty. These heresies were essentially a denial of original sin and the belief that one can live without sin apart from the grace of Christ. Caelestius was called to a council in Carthage in 411 but refused to recant. He moved to Ephesus where he was ordained. His ideas remained popular in North Africa however, causing Augustine to write many treatises against this new error he called Pelagianism.

Pelagius himself continued to write in the East.[21] He was called to a council in Jerusalem in 415 but was found innocent at it.[22] This has caused many scholars to think of the objection to Pelagianism as specifically western.[23] However, there does still seem to have been significant objection to Pelagianism in the East, as Caelestius fled from Ephesus around this time.[24] While the reasons for this are not known for certain, it was likely due to reactions to his Pelagian views. Caelestius ended up moving to Constantinople, but the bishop expelled him from the city for heresy.[25]

Another council was called in Carthage in 419.[26] This council would come to be seen as one of the most definitive condemnations of Pelagianism, as it received papal approval. Some of the canons regarding Pelagianism are as follows: [27]

---

[20] Joseph Pohle, "Pelagius and Pelagianism," in *The Catholic Encyclopedia*, vol. 11., (New York: Robert Appleton Company, 1911), rev. and ed. for New Advent by Kevin Knight, https://www.newadvent.org/cathen/11604a.htm.

[21] Pohle.

[22] Scholl, 109.

[23] Scholl, 98-107.

[24] Scholl, 113-14.

[25] Scholl, 110.

[26] Pohle.

[27] "Council of Carthage (A.D. 419)," in *The Seven Ecumenical Councils*. trans. Henry Percival, (Buffalo, NY: Christian Literature Publishing Co., 1900), 109-112.

Canon 109

That whosoever says that Adam, the first man, was created mortal, so that whether he had sinned or not, he would have died in body — that is, he would have gone forth of the body, not because his sin merited this, but by natural necessity, let him be anathema.

Canon 110

Likewise it seemed good that whosoever denies that infants newly from their mother's wombs should be baptized, or says that baptism is for remission of sins, but that they derive from Adam no original sin, which needs to be removed by the laver of regeneration, from whence the conclusion follows, that in them the form of baptism for the remission of sins, is to be understood as false and not true, let him be anathema.

For no otherwise can be understood what the Apostle says, "By one man sin has come into the world, and death through sin, and so death passed upon all men in that all have sinned," [Rom 5:12] than the Catholic Church everywhere diffused has always understood it. For on account of this rule of faith even infants, who could have committed as yet no sin themselves, therefore are truly baptized for the remission of sins, in order that what in them is the result of generation may be cleansed by regeneration.

Canon 112

Also, whoever shall say that the same grace of God through Jesus Christ our Lord helps us only in not sinning by revealing to us and opening to our understanding the commandments, so that we may know what to seek, what we ought to avoid, and also that we should love to do so, but that through it we are not helped so that we are able to do what we know we should do, let him be anathema. For when the Apostle says: "Wisdom puffs up, but charity edifies" [1 Cor 8:1] it were truly infamous were we to believe that we have the grace of Christ for that which puffs us up, but have it not for that which edifies, since in each case it is the gift of God, both to know what we ought to do, and to love to do it; so that wisdom cannot puff us up while charity is edifying us. For as of God it is written, "Who teaches man knowledge," [Ps 94:10] so also it is written, "Love is of God" [1 Jn 4:7].

The main focus of these canons was condemnation of denying original sin and denying that grace is necessary for salvation. The use of Romans 5:12 in canon 110 is important as it shows that this verse was key in the condemnation of Pelagianism. However, just because this verse was quoted at the council does not mean it was the only verse underlying the theology of original sin presented here.

While Pelagius himself died in 418, Pelagianism did not fully die out.[28] Julian of Eclanum, an Italian bishop, continued to promote Pelagianism. This led Augustine to continue to write against Pelagianism. Meanwhile, Caelestius moved to Constantinople again.[29] The new bishop, Nestorius, welcomed Caelestius. However, a few years later, both Caelestius and Nestorius were condemned as heretics at the Council of Ephesus in 431, finally anathematizing Pelagianism at an ecumenical level.

The condemnation of Pelagianism in the East as well as its connection to Nestorianism shows that the East was no more sympathetic to Pelagianism than the West was. Pelagianism was rarely talked about after this in the East, but this is no surprise given that most of the writing on the matter were in Latin and that Pelagianism only continued to be an issue after this in the West.[30]

III. Augustine's View of Original Sin

As mentioned above, Augustine was the main theological opponent of Pelagianism. While there were many different doctrines of Pelagianism which Augustine opposed, key among them was original sin. At original sin lay the real core of the dispute. Pelagius held that man from birth had a "natural sanctity" to do good works.[31] This ultimately allowed man to be saved without the need of grace. In order to argue that man needs grace, Augustine had to establish that man needs grace from the moment of birth. This would lead him to write frequently about original sin.

Despite Augustine's copious writings on the matter, his views are often misunderstood.[32] Although Romanides and Meyendorff make the claim that Augustine held that all humans, even infants, as personally guilty and worthy of damnation for the sin of Adam, a close reading of Augustine reveals far more nuance in his thought.

One difficulty with understanding Augustine's thoughts on the matter is that they evolved over the course of his life.[33] Later students

---

[28] Pohle.

[29] Scholl, 112.

[30] Pohle.

[31] Pelagius, *Ad Demetriadem*, 4.2, quoted in Scholl, 36.

[32] Jesse Couenhoven, "St. Augustine's Doctrine of Original Sin," *Augustinian Studies* 36, no. 2 (2005): 359.

[33] Nathaniel McCallum, "Inherited Guilt in Saints Augustine and Cyril," 2016,

of Augustine in the centuries to come would even quote his own works from different points in his life against one another. However, there are overarching themes and a general agreement, especially if one reads carefully. As Augustine debated the Pelagians, his theology matured and became more nuanced, but the same core doctrines remained.

Augustine did believe in inherited sin.[34] However, he is very nuanced on what he means by this. He is clear that they do not hold personal sin, since one can only be held personally guilty for a sin that they themselves have committed.[35] In his initial debates, with the Pelagians, Augustine makes this distinction through his terminology. There are three terms that Augustine uses for sin, *culpa, reatus,* and *reus*.[36] These terms come from Roman legal language. *Culpa* is usually translated as "fault." *Reatus* and *reus* are both usually translated as guilt, but there is a slight difference in the Latin.[37] *Reus* refers to the person accused or convicted of a crime, while *reatus* refers to the condition of being *reus*.

Due to the similarity of meanings, Augustine initially uses these terms interchangeably.[38] However, when Augustine actually starts debating the Pelagians, he begins to be very careful to nuance his terms.[39] At this point, he uses *reus* and *culpa* only for personal sin. *Reatus* is the only word used for the guilt of original sin. Augustine uses it as a "liability for punishment... which is remitted in baptism."[40] Later on though, Augustine is forced to stop this as Julian brings up earlier biblical and patristic witnesses who did not make this careful linguistic distinction.[41] One specific issue was the translation of Romans 3:19 in the old Latin translations, which rendered ὑπόδικος (liable for trial) as *reus*.[42] As a result, Augustine stops making the same linguistic distinctions. However, he still maintains the same theology, arguing to Julian that "no matter whence born, a man is

---

https://www.academia.edu/29213788/Inherited_Guilt_in_Saints_Augustine_and_Cyril, 3-9.

[34] Couenhoven, 370.

[35] Couenhoven, 362; McCallum, 3-9.

[36] McCallum, 4.

[37] McCallum, 4-5.

[38] McCallum, 4-5.

[39] McCallum, 6-7.

[40] McCallum, 7.

[41] McCallum, 8-9.

[42] The Vulgate instead renders it as *subditus*. McCallum, 8.

innocent because there is no personal sin, and he is *reum* through original sin."[43]

Augustine specifies what type of guilt this is; it is concupiscence.[44] This is the state of disordered desire which everyone is born with.[45] He repeatedly calls it a "carnal concupiscence," as it arises from the desires of the flesh.[46] He considers it sin itself in the sense that it urges one to sin.[47]

Meyendorff considers one major difference that Augustine's views on original sin led him to is that infants are damned.[48] This is an accurate portrayal of Augustine's views. In fact, Augustine rejects any sort of middle, third place to which infants could go.[49] His reasoning is that since they are not baptized, they are not part of the faithful, and would suffer "the wrath of God" along with all other heathens. However, the later western tradition did not entirely follow Augustine on this point. While there was still a common belief that infants went to hell, the later tradition held that no suffering was inflicted upon unbaptized infants. Augustine himself came to be interpreted this way as well, based on Augustine's very own distinction between personal guilt and original guilt.[50]

Augustine is uncertain in exactly what sense the sin of Adam is present in infants. Drawing on 1 Corinthians 15:22, he does consider the relationship of Adam to Christ as type to antitype.[51] He also later bolsters this with Romans 5:12, but not initially. As a result of this typology and these scriptural verses, Augustine concludes that "we all

---

[43] Augustine, *Against Julian*, trans. Matthew A. Schumacher, (Washington: Catholic University of America Press, 2013), 153.

[44] Couenhoven, 372-81.

[45] Couenhoven, 371.

[46] c.f. Couenhoven, 371-76.

[47] Couenhoven, 376-77. Couenhoven himself thinks Augustine at sometimes held it as personal sin itself but says that he thinks Augustine's overall view is "to hold that carnal concupiscence, even if it is not acted on, or out of, is itself sin, and [Couenhoven] take[s] this to be [Augustine's] settled position."

[48] Meyendorff, 145.

[49] Augustine, *A Treatise on the Merit and Forgiveness of Sins, and the Baptism of Infants*, in *Nicene and Post-Nicene Fathers, First Series*, vol. 5. trans. Peter Holmes and Robert Ernest Wallis, rev. Benjamin B. Warfield, (Buffalo, NY: Christian Literature Publishing Co., 1887), 1.28.

[50] c.f. Thomas Aquinas, *The Summa Theologiae*, 2nd and rev. ed., trans. Fathers of the English Dominican Province, online ed. ed. Kevin Knight, 2017, https://www.newadvent.org/summa/, Supp.69.6.reply.2.

[51] Couenhoven, 362-63.

were in that one man" and so from birth we are "vitiated by sin, and bound by the chain of death, and justly condemned."[52] However, Augustine is not entirely sure in what sense humans were in Adam. He says specifically in that same passage that humans were in Adam in a "seminal nature." He himself is not entirely sure what he means by this though and wavered back and forth between the views that each soul is created fallen, that it is matter which passes sin on, or that the soul itself comes from the souls of the parents, although he found issues with all these stances.[53] Augustine held the doctrine must be believed regardless though on the basis that it is taught in scripture, taught by earlier fathers, and is seen in the sacramental life of the Church.

Romanides misunderstands what Augustine means by all humans being "in Adam." He takes Augustine to mean that "in some way, Adam's will was inherited by his descendants."[54] Romanides cites *On the Grace of Christ, and on Original Sin* 2.48 as proof, but this passage says nothing of inheriting will.[55] As already pointed out above, Augustine's views are much more nuanced. All humans are present in Christ, and one is only personally held guilty of sins committed by one's own will, but this does not mean that the will is itself inherited, since there is a secondary form of guilt, original guilt, which is not

---

[52] Augustine, *The City of God*, in *Nicene and Post-Nicene Fathers, First Series*, vol. 2, trans. Marcus Dods. ed. Philip Schaff, (Buffalo, NY: Christian Literature Publishing Co., 1887), 13.14.

[53] Couenhoven, 383-86.

[54] Romanides, 23.

[55] "These words, however, of the man of God are contradicted by Pelagius, notwithstanding all his commendation of his author, when he himself declares that 'we are procreated, as without virtue, so without vice.' What remains, then, but that Pelagius should condemn and renounce this error of his; or else be sorry that he has quoted Ambrose in the way he has? Inasmuch, however, as the blessed Ambrose, catholic bishop as he is, has expressed himself in the above-quoted passages in accordance with the catholic faith, it follows that Pelagius, along with his disciple Cœlestius, was justly condemned by the authority of the catholic Church for having turned aside from the true way of faith, since he repented not for having bestowed commendation on Ambrose, and for having at the same time entertained opinions in opposition to him. I know full well with what insatiable avidity you read whatever is written for edification and in confirmation of the faith; but yet, notwithstanding its utility as contributing to such an end, I must at last bring this treatise to a conclusion." Augustine, *A Treatise on the Grace of Christ, and on Original Sin*, in *Nicene and Post-Nicene Fathers, First Series*, vol. 5, trans. Peter Holmes and Robert Ernest Wallis, rev. Benjamin B. Warfield, ed. Philip Schaff, (Buffalo, NY: Christian Literature Publishing Co., 1887.), 2.48.

personal.

Romanides here attributed to Augustine what is actually the view of John Calvin.[56] It is Calvin who thinks that the individual sin of Adam is imputed to the sinner, making him personally guilty. For Augustine, it is an ontological participation in Adam that brings original sin. This is because Adam represents human nature, and so he "made only the nature guilty."[57] Nathaniel McCallum points out that "in this passage that there is a seamless blending of the medical and legal terminologies that Meyendorff wishes to juxtapose."[58] One major problem with the interpretations of Romanides and Meyendorff is that they read Augustine as though here were a Calvinist, but Augustine's views must be taken on his own terms.

One other critique of Romanides must be considered here. According to Romanides, Augustine believed that the end of human life was a mere "*eudaimonia*" like in Aristotle, rather than the Eastern patristic doctrine of θέωσις, or divinization.[59] In actuality, what Augustine is denying is merely Pelagius' understanding of divinization.[60] He instead views divinization as a radically divine process. It is God alone who gives grace and saves, and so it is God who divinizes man. This is in complete opposition to both Neoplatonism and Pelagianism. Romanides thinks that Augustine misunderstood original sin because he misunderstood its larger context, but this is a misreading of Augustine.

IV. Possible Meanings of Romans 5:12

Since it is now clear what Augustine taught about original sin, it is now important to look at if it is novel. Since Romanides and Meyendorff both say that Romans 5:12 was the key verse in this controversy, this is the most important lens through which to view the doctrine. In this verse, Paul says,

Διὰ τοῦτο ὥσπερ δι' ἑνὸς ἀνθρώπου ἡ ἁμαρτία εἰς τὸν κόσμον εἰσῆλθεν καὶ διὰ τῆς ἁμαρτίας ὁ θάνατος, καὶ οὕτως εἰς πάντας ἀνθρώπους ὁ θάνατος διῆλθεν, ἐφ' ᾧ πάντες ἥμαρτον.

Therefore as through one man sin came into the world and through sin

---

[56] Couenhoven, 370-71.
[57] Augustine, *Against Julian*, 117.
[58] McCallum, 8; c.f. Meyendorff, 146.
[59] Romanides, 103-11.
[60] Scholl, 24-57.

death, therefore also death spread to all men, *in whom* all have sinned.

As mentioned above, Augustine takes this verse to mean that in the person of Adam, all have sinned. This is because of the rendering of ἐφ' ᾧ as *in quo* in Augustine's Latin copy of Romans. However, according to Romanides and Meyendorff that this is not what St. Paul meant by the phrase. Fr. Joseph Fitzmyer lists 11 different translations of ἐφ' ᾧ that have been suggested.[61] Of these, a few are important to examine: "in whom," "because of whom," "because of which [death]," and "with the result that."

Romanides and Meyendorff take ἐφ' ᾧ to mean "because of which," that is "because of death." This is certainly grammatically possible because ὁ θάνατος is masculine. It is also the most immediate antecedent to the relative. However, it is unclear how death would cause sin since after one has died, they can no longer sin. Romanides and Meyendorff take the death here to only be a tendency towards death, a corruptibility, but Paul nowhere indicates this. In addition, Fitzmyer points out that this interpretation is inconsistent with Paul's other statements on the matter, such as Romans 5:21 and 6:23, where Paul places death as the result of sin.[62]

Augustine himself makes this point, saying that "all die in the sin; they do not sin in the death; for when sin precedes, death follows — not when death precedes, sin follows. Because sin is the sting of death."[63] Augustine instead suggests that "Adam" should be understood as what the relative refers to, since it cannot be "sin" since "in Greek, from which the Epistle is translated, sin is expressed in the feminine gender." He does acknowledge the grammatical possibility of "death" since "death in the Greek language is of the masculine gender," but rejects it on the hermeneutical grounds explained above. This also shows that Augustine was well aware of the Greek grammatical issues at play here from others, even if his own Greek was not very good.

"Because of whom" is the translation that Meyendorff suggests

---

61 Joseph A. Fitzmyer, *Romans: A New Translation with Introduction and Commentary*, (New York: Doubleday, 1993), 413-17.
62 Fitzmyer, 414.
63 Augustine, *Against Two Letters of the Pelagians*, in *Nicene and Post-Nicene Fathers, First Series*, vol. 5, trans. Peter Holmes and Robert Ernest Wallis, rev. Benjamin B. Warfield, ed. Philip Schaff. (Buffalo, NY: Christian Literature Publishing Co., 1887), 4.7.

most scholars follow.[64] He cites Fitzmyer to prove this.[65] However, Meyendorff is actually incorrect about Fitzmyer's own views. Fitzmyer himself translates ἐφ' ᾧ as "with the result that."[66] He takes Paul to be "expressing a result, the sequel to Adam's baneful influence on humanity by the ratification of his sin in the sins of all individuals." This would certainly place some responsibility for death onto individuals, closer to the views of Romanides and Meyendorff, but it still would not be enough to undermine the theology of Augustine since it would still put the main responsibility for sin onto Adam. As Fitzmyer points out, "the fate of humanity ultimately rests on what its head, Adam, has done to it." Indeed, he thinks that Augustine's theology of original sin is correct, only that this is the wrong verse to appeal to, since "the primary causality for its sinful condition is ascribed to Adam, no matter what meaning is assigned to *eph' hō*." Fitzmyer suggests that v. 15-19 are actually a better proof text of original sin and that the paragraph must be taken as a whole. Fitzmyer's interpretation does pose its own challenges though. He is forced to add in a two-fold causality for death, but Paul nowhere states this. In order to assert this interpretation, further evidence would be needed that Paul held death to have a two-fold cause. No matter which of these translations is taken though, all of them still allow for an Augustinian understanding of original sin.

The best defense of "because of whom" is given by Fr. Domenico Palmieri. Palmieri argues this on the basis of the usage of ἐφ' ᾧ in 2 Corinthians 5:4 and Philippians 3:12.[67]

> καὶ γὰρ οἱ ὄντες ἐν τῷ σκήνει στενάζομεν βαρούμενοι, *ἐφ' ᾧ* οὐ θέλομεν ἐκδύσασθαι...

> For also while being in the body we sigh anxiously, not *because of which* we wish to be unclothed... (2 Cor 5:4).[68]

> ...διώκω δὲ εἰ καὶ καταλάβω, *ἐφ' ᾧ* καὶ κατελήμφθην ὑπὸ Χριστοῦ.

> ...but I push forward in order that I might lay hold of it, *because* I was laid hold of by Christ (Phil 3:12).

These verses certainly lend weight to Palmieri's interpretation.

---

[64] Meyendorff, 144.

[65] Meyendorff, 149-50.

[66] Fitzmyer, 416-17.

[67] Dominicus Palmieri, *Tractatus De Peccato Originali et De Immaculato Beatae Virginis Deiparae Conceptu*, (Romae: Typ. Iuvenum Opificum A S. Iosepho, 1904), 18-19.

[68] Palmieri writes in Latin, so the English translations here are my own.

Fitzmyer and Palmieri also note that this is the general way the preposition is taken by the Greek Fathers.[69] However, "because of whom" is really not that much different from "in whom." In both cases, it is Adam's sin which is the reason all men have sin. The only difference is whether or not men are actually in Adam at the fall.

Fitzmyer's primary objections to "in whom" is that Paul would have used ἐν ᾧ instead, like he does in 1 Corinthians 15:22, and that "ἑνὸς ἀνθρώπου" is too far from "ᾧ" for it to be referring to Adam, the "one man."[70] However, these can be explained. First, mere difference of phrasing does not necessarily show a difference in meaning. Indeed, 1 Corinthians 15:22 was the other main verse appealed to in the Pelagian controversy and Meyendorff himself thinks that Romans 5:12 should be interpreted in light of this verse.[71] Paul's theology should be understood as a unitary whole, and so it makes sense to interpret Romans 5:12 in light of 1 Corinthians 15:22. Secondly, the fact that "ἑνὸς ἀνθρώπου" is far from "ᾧ" is not proof that the latter cannot refer to the former. The fact they are in the same sentence leaves it as a likely possibility. Even if it were a difficulty, it still is not certain proof. If the evidence were to suggest that "ᾧ" refers to "ἑνὸς ἀνθρώπου," then their separation by a mere 19 words would not be enough to suggest otherwise. As shown, any interpretation poses some interpretive challenge, and this one seems very minor compared to the other challenges. It seems then that "in whom" or "because of whom" are the best possible interpretations, and these are close in meaning. An analysis of Paul's Jewish context may help provide some weight to the former.

V. Romans 5:12 in its Jewish Context

Augustine's interpretation of Romans 5:12 is based upon the notion of corporate personhood. Corporate personhood is the idea that one person can represent a whole group of people. It is frequently thought that Augustine's notion of corporate personhood is Platonic and would therefore be foreign to St. Paul. Meyendorff actually accepts a notion of corporate personhood as it is in St. Gregory of Nyssa, and so he should have no issue with Augustine going in this

---

[69] Fitzmyer, 414; Palmieri, 22-26.
[70] Fitzmyer, 414.
[71] Couenhoven, 662-363; McCallum, 5; Meyendorff, 143-44.

direction.[72] However, since some may object that Gregory of Nyssa's interpretation is foreign to the New Testament, it will be worth examining the concept of corporate personhood in second temple Judaism to see if the concept would have actually been foreign to Paul.[73]

In the Old Testament, it is actually very frequent that an ancestor represents his whole people. Israel is frequently referred to with respect to its relation as "the seed (*zèra'*) of Abraham" (Isa. 41:8; c.f. Josh. 24:2).[74] In fact, the name Israel itself refers to the descent of the people of Israel from Jacob who was renamed Israel by God (Gen. 32:28). The Israelites are very frequently also called the "seed of Jacob" and the "seed of Israel" (Ps. 21:24; Isa. 43:5; 44:3, 45:19, 25, 48:19; 54:3; Jer. 31:36, 33:26, 37; 46:27). Likewise, the various tribes are called by the names of the children of Jacob. The priestly line is referred to as "Aaron and his seed" or the "line of Zadok" (Exo. 28:43; 30:21; Lev. 21:17; 22:3-4; Num. 17:5; Eze. 43:19; 1 Mac. 7:14).

Besides seed, "sons of (*b^en é*)" is also frequently used to show corporate personhood through ancestry.[75] Fr. Jean de Fraine suggests that *bén* is etymologically related to *bānāh*, to build. It is frequently used to describe building a house. Sometimes, this building is in a metaphorical sense, such as building a metaphorical house, a family (Gen 16:22; 1 Sam 2:35; 1 King. 11:38; Ruth 4:11). De Fraine suggests that the etymological relation is that "each *bén* is in intimate and structural relationship with a 'father,' of whom he is a participation of an individual expression." The concept of corporate personhood through ancestry is therefore firmly rooted in the Hebrew language itself.

This corporate personhood through ancestry is applied to Adam as well. In fact, *'ādām ha'ādām* (with the article) more frequently mean "mankind" or "anyone" than "Adam" (Gen 6:6, 7; 8:21; Lev. 1:2; 5:3-4; Ps. 143:3-4; Ecc. 1:3; 6:12; Job 14:1, 10; 28:28; 34:15; Sir. 15:17; Isa. 6:12; Jer. 10:23; Mic. 6:8).[76] "Son of Adam (*bèn-'ādam*)"

---

[72] John Meyendorff, *Byzantine Theology: Historical Trends and Doctrinal Themes*, (New York: Fordham University Press, 1987), 143-44.

[73] For a fuller study of corporate personhood in the Old Testament, see Jean de Fraine, *Adam and the Family of Man*, trans. (Daniel Raible. Staten Island: Alba House, 1965).

[74] de Fraine, 126-27. The possible biblical examples are far too many to list, so the lists here is simply the ones provided by de Fraine.

[75] de Fraine, 129-34.

[76] de Fraine, 134-39. This is again only a small fraction of the possible examples.

and "sons of Adam (*b^e^né-'ādām*)" are also frequently used to refer to a person, group of people, or all of mankind (Num. 23:19; 1 King. 8:39; 2 Chr. 6:30; Ps. 44:2; 57:2; 145:3; Pro. 8:31; Jer. 49:18, 33; Eze. 2:6, 8; 3:25; 4:1, Dan 6:17).[77]

Beyond merely the biblical examples, the concept of humanity as present in Adam at the fall was common in the second temple Jewish context that Paul lived in.[78] The clearest example of this is 4 Esdras.[79] The author of 4 Esdras follows Paul in asserting that death is the result of sin, stating that God "imposed a single precept on him [Adam], but he transgressed it. Immediately [God] condemned him and his descendants to death" (4 Esd. 3:7). The author of 4 Esdras here denies a mere spiritual death brought about by sin. The first sin causes death "immediately." He clarifies though that it is not merely death that was brought in, but a change in the disposition of men, concupiscence, by saying that "because of his evil heart Adam fall into sin and guilt; the same thing takes place in all of those born of him... The Law was indeed present in the hearts of the people, but the evil seed was also present" (4 Esd. 3:21). Later, the author of 4 Esdras brings in a closer connection between Adam and all of mankind by stating that "when you [Adam] sinned, your fall affected not only you but us, your descendants" (4 Esd. 7:118). From these three passages, it is clear that the author of 4 Esdras held that Adam's sin brought in death and concupiscence to all mankind, implanting an "evil seed" in people's hearts.

Another example of corporate personhood in second temple Judaism is *The Apocalypse of Baruch*.[80] It suggests the possibility of the presence of all of man in Adam at the fall, saying that "when Adam sinned and when the sentence of death was pronounced on all those who would descend from him, the number of those born was fixed as was the place of the sojourn for the living and the dead" (23:4). This suggests the corporate personhood of Adam in two ways. First, when Adam is sentenced, all of mankind is sentenced. This implies they must have been in him in some way. There is also the judicial language reflected in Augustine present here. Secondly, the number who would live and where they would go even after death was predestined here at the fall. This is a very Augustinian idea, although Augustine believed

---

[77] de Fraine, 140-42.
[78] de Fraine, 146-49.
[79] Also commonly known as 2 Esdras, such as in the KJV.
[80] de Fraine, 146-47

that it is in Christ, the second Adam, that men are predestined. Still, the concept of a predestination in Adam suggests a corporate existence in Adam. Some parts of the *Apocalypse of Baruch* do seem less Augustinian. For example, it says that "Adam was the first sinner and brought premature death upon all, his descendants have brought upon themselves future punishment or glorification" (54:15). Here the author of the *Apocalypse of Baruch* explicitly denies that men are guilty of Adam's sin. However, this need not necessarily be read as entirely contrary to Augustine. After all, Augustine does not deny that people are punished for their own sins. It does show though that while reading Paul as holding corporate personhood is entirely within the Jewish tradition, there is diversity in second temple Judaism as to how this corporate personhood is to be understood. It is also important to note that he takes the death brought in by Adam to be a literal, not merely spiritual death. Indeed, the concept that Adam's sin merely brought spiritual death is entirely absent from second temple Jewish thought.

Rabbinic literature also reflects the corporate personhood of Adam. For example, in *Midrash Coheleth* 43, when God tells Moses that he must die, Moses asks "'Because of what sin?' And God replied to him, 'Because of the sin of the first Adam'" (ad. 7:13).[81] Men have to die because Adam committed a sin. This seems to suggest in some sense *Midrash Coheleth* 43 holds everyone in some sense, even if not personally, guilty of the sin of Adam and so sentenced to death because of it. Other rabbinic literature goes even further with the corporate personhood of Adam. One passage of *Yalkut Shemeoni* teaches that when God made Adam, He "summed up the entire creation in him."[82] In this example, Adam is not only the corporate representative of mankind, but all of creation. Paul echoes a similar sentiment (c.f. Rom. 8:22).

The corporate personhood based on ancestry is present in much of the New Testament. *Bèn-'ādam* is used in the New Testament frequently as Son of Man (ὁ υἱὸς τοῦ ἀνθρώπου) to refer to Jesus. In the Aramaic which Jesus spoke, may have been calling Himself "Son of Adam."[83] The Gospel of John specifically is full of language of

---

[81] de Fraine, 148.

[82] de Fraine, 149.

[83] While the most famous use of "Son of man" in the Hebrew Bible does not use *bèn-'ādam* (Dan 7:13), most other instances of the phrase do, such as Dan 8:17 and most uses of it in Ezekiel.

corporate personhood, calling his followers the true "seed of Abraham (σπέρμα Ἀβραάμ)" and "children of Abraham (τέκνα τοῦ Ἀβραάμ)" (John 8:36-41). Finally, the author to the Hebrews also refers to the Israelites as "in the loins (ὀσφύϊ)" of Abraham (Heb. 7:10).

VI. Original Sin in the Church Fathers

Despite its great importance in the New Testament, original sin is not a widely discussed topic in the ante-Nicene fathers. Among the apostolic fathers there is essentially no discussion.[84] However, it quickly does become a topic of interest.

One early father to discuss the topic was St. Irenaeus. Irenaeus is one of Romanides' main sources, being mentioned on 56 pages.[85] Romanides claims that Irenaeus holds that "ᾧ" in Romans 5:12 referred to death, not sin.[86] This would be impossible to know though, given that Irenaeus does not cite the verse a single time in his entire extant corpus.[87]

Romanides also claims that Irenaeus "uses the phrase 'because of death' (ἐπί [sic] τῷ θανάτῳ) etiologically." However, the phrase "ἐπὶ τῷ θανάτῳ"[88] does not appear in any extant work of Irenaeus. Romanides cites one example from the Βιβλιοθήκη Ἑλλήνων Πατέρων καὶ Ἐκκλησιαστικῶν Συγγραφέων.[89] However, the fragment Romanides quotes is not considered authentic. Indeed, it is so certainly inauthentic that the *Clavis Patrum Graecorum* does not even bother to include it with a note of spuriousness.[90] Even if the quote is authentic though, it does not prove discontinuity with Augustine. Romanides claims that Irenaeus says that "the passions that have naturally befallen us because of death; I refer to grief and cowardice and perplexity, distress and all the rest by which our nature afflicted with death and corruptibility is known."[91] It is not at all clear here that Irenaeus is

---

[84] David Weaver, "From Paul to Augustine: Romans 5:12 in Early Christian Exegesism," *St. Vladimir's Theological Quarterly* 27, no. 3 (1983): 189.

[85] Romanides, 186.

[86] Romanides, 167.

[87] According to the Thesaurus Linguae Graecae.

[88] I have corrected the accent on "ἐπί" to the grave here.

[89] Romanides. 167.

[90] Mauritii Geerard, *Clavis Patrum Graecorum: Patres Antenicaeni,* vol. 1, (Turnhout: Brepols. 1983), 1315.

[91] Irenaeus, *Fragment* 52b, ΒΕΠΕΣ, vol. 5, (Athens: Ἀποστολική Διακονία, 1955), 186, quoted in Romanides 167.

intending this as an interpretation of Romans 5:12. It is not under dispute that the fall brought about the passions according to the Fathers.

Elsewhere, Irenaeus is very clear about the order: sin brought about death. He says that Eve "having become disobedient, was made the cause of death, both to herself and to the whole human race."[92] It is through the first sin that death entered the world then. While here Irenaeus names Eve, he elsewhere names Adam as the cause of death.[93] He only names Eve here because his context is a defense of Mary as the second Eve. Irenaeus in fact explicitly teaches the corporate personhood of Adam at the fall. He says that "we had offended [God] in the first Adam, when he did not perform His commandment."[94] All people have offended God in Adam. This is very close to Augustine's view that all people are guilty in Adam.

It is worth noting that this more developed view of original sin was not universally held in the second century. Neither St. Theophilus of Antioch nor St. Justin Martyr affirm the transmission of sin to infants.[95] However, both do affirm that Adam's sin is the cause of death in the world. Indeed, this is one of the central arguments in Justin's *Dialogue with Trypho*. These fathers then can still be said to hold the doctrine albeit it not fully. Their view was certainly not universal though, as shown by the example of Irenaeus. Justin and Theophilus ought not to be read in isolation, but within the larger context of the *consensus patrum*.

In the next century, original sin can be seen quite clearly in Origen.[96] In reflecting upon numerous scriptural verses, particularly the purification of women after birth, Origen notes that "only sinners rejoice over their birthday" while the saints "curse that day."[97] This is because "every soul which is born is polluted with the filth 'of iniquity

---

[92] Irenaeus, *Against Heresies*, in *Ante-Nicene Fathers*, vol. 1, trans. Alexander Roberts and William Rambaut, ed. Alexander Roberts, James Donaldson, and A. Cleveland Coxe, (Buffalo, NY: Christian Literature Publishing Co., 1885.), 3.22.4.

[93] c.f. Irenaeus, *Against Heresies*, 3.23.

[94] Irenaeus, *Against Heresies*, 5.16.3.

[95] Weaver, 189-91.

[96] Adam G. Cooper, "Sex and the Transmission of Sin: Patristics Exegesis of Psalm 50:5 (LXX)," in *Meditations of the Heart: The Psalms in Early Christian Thought and Practice*, ed. Andreas Andreopoulos, Augustine Casiday, and Carol Harrison, (Turnhout: Brepolis, 2011), 83-85.

[97] Origen, *Homilies on Leviticus, 1-16*, trans. Gary Wayne Barkley, (Washington: The Catholic University of America Press, 200), 8.3.2.

and sin.' [Psalm 51:5]"[98] As additional evidence, Origen points out that the Church baptizes infants, and "if there were nothing in infants that ought to pertain to forgiveness and indulgence, then the grace of baptism would appear superfluous." In a homily upon this same Levitical purification ritual in Luke, Origen develops a distinction between "*sordes*" (stain) and "*peccatum*" (sin).[99] Babies are born with *sordes* but not *peccatum*. This is very similar to in meaning to Augustine's later distinction between *reatus* and *reus*.[100] Infants are born with some sort of stain, but it is distinct from personal sins. Palmieri also points out that when Origen uses Romans 5:12, he takes "ἐφ' ᾧ to refer to Adam."[101] Although the Church came to reject Origen's belief in the preexistence of souls, this is not essential to Origen's views on original sin since the preexistence of souls was just Origen's method of explaining how all of humanity was present in Adam.[102] This particular metaphysical explanation is not necessary for the doctrine expressed here.

Contemporary with Origen, St. Cyprian also uses baptism to prove the need of infants to receive baptism for the remission of original sin.[103] Cyprian says that a newborn "has not sinned, except in that, being born after the flesh according to Adam, he has contracted the contagion of the ancient death at its earliest birth."[104] In infant baptism then is "remitted, not his own sins, but the sins of another." This is nearly identical to what Augustine would write in the same region a century and a half later. As early as the third century then, the transmission of sin to newborns was nearly universally held.

Tertullian also witnesses to original sin in the third century, especially the corporate personhood of Christ. Tertullian distinguishes between the soul as initially "in Adam until it is born again in

---

[98] Origen, *Homilies on Leviticus*, 8.3.5.

[99] Origen, *Homilies on Luke*, trans. Joseph T. Lienhard, (Washington: The Catholic University of America Press, 2009), 14.3. The homily is unfortunately only extant in Latin, but it was originally written in Greek. Lienhard, xxi.

[100] Cooper, 84.

[101] Palmieri, 22; c.f. Origen, *Homilies on Numbers*, trans. Thomas P. Scheck, ed. Christopher A. Hall, (Downers Grove: Intervarsity Press, 2009), *Numbers* 22.3.3.

[102] Cooper, 84-85.

[103] Cooper, 85-86.

[104] Cyprian, *The Epistles of Cyprian*, in *Ante-Nicene Fathers*, vol. 5, trans. Robert Ernest Wallis, ed. Alexander Roberts, James Donaldson, and A. Cleveland Coxe, (Buffalo, NY: Christian Literature Publishing Co., 1886), 58.5.

Christ."[105] This shows Tertullian's view of the corporate personhood of Adam. Tertullian's reasoning for this was that the "soul (which may be compared with the nascent sprout of a tree) has been derived from Adam as its root."[106] Although the Church came to depart from Tertullian's traducianism, he is an important witness to the corporate personhood of Adam in the early Church. Like Origen, Tertullian's particular metaphysical explanation is not necessary to uphold the doctrine he expresses here.

The Eastern Fathers from Augustine's own time of the fourth and fifth centuries are also in agreement with Augustine. St. Gregory of Nyssa's writings on original sin are strikingly close to Augustine.[107] Speaking of the exile from paradise, he says that all men "in our first ancestor were thus ejected."[108] The corporate personhood of Adam is central to Gregory's theology. He explains this corporate personhood by saying that through Adam's fall "death had been mingled with human nature."[109] This finally allows for an explanation of the corporate personhood of Adam without leading into the heresies of the preexistence of souls or traducianism. Adam represents all of human nature. The fall causes one to have a fallen nature because they are in the nature that Adam has. Christ is the second Adam and offers a redeemed human nature to all men.

St. Basil and St. Gregory Nazianzen also speaks of the corporate personhood of Adam in similar language. Basil talks of the whole human race being present in Adam before the fall, saying that "we were once glorious when we lived in Paradise."[110] Likewise, Gregory speaks about how all men have "wholly sinned and was condemned

---

[105] Tertullian, *A Treatise on the Soul* in *Ante-Nicene Fathers*, vol. 3, trans. Peter Holmes, ed. Alexander Roberts, James Donaldson, and A. Cleveland Coxe, (Buffalo, NY: Christian Literature Publishing Co., 1886), 40.

[106] Tertullian, 19.

[107] For a more detailed account of Gregory of Nyssa's theology of original sin, see Ernest V. McClear, "The Fall of Man and Original Sin in the Theology of Gregory of Nyssa," *Theological Studies* 9, no. 2 (1948): 175-212.

[108] Gregory of Nyssa, *On Virginity*, in *Nicene and Post-Nicene Fathers, Second Series*, vol. 5, trans. William Moore and Henry Austin Wilson, ed. Philip Schaff and Henry Wace, (Buffalo, NY: Christian Literature Publishing Co., 1893), 12.

[109] Gregory of Nyssa, *Homilies on the Song of Songs*, trans. Richard A. Noris Jr., ed. Brian E. Daley and John T. Fitzgerald, (Atlanta: Society of Biblical Literature, 2012), 12.351.

[110] Basil, *Commentary on the Psalms*, 114.5, quoted in Cooper, 89.

through the disobedience of the first-formed."[111] The Cappadocians all hold the same theology that it is through human nature that all of humanity was present at the fall, to the point that they even feel free to speak of themselves as being there in the first person.

While the Cappadocians do not go as far as Augustine to declare that infants are damned, they do come close. Gregory Nazianzen for example, when speaking of infant baptism, says,

> Others are not in a position to receive it, perhaps on account of infancy, or some perfectly involuntary circumstance through which they are prevented from receiving it, even if they wish. As then in the former case we found much difference, so too in this. They who altogether despise it are worse than they who neglect it through greed or carelessness. These are worse than they who have lost the Gift through ignorance or tyranny, for tyranny is nothing but an involuntary error. And I think that the first will have to suffer punishment, as for all their sins, so for their contempt of baptism; and that the second will also have to suffer, but less, because it was not so much through wickedness as through folly that they wrought their failure; and that the third will be neither glorified nor punished by the righteous Judge, as unsealed and yet not wicked, but persons who have suffered rather than done wrong. For not every one who is not bad enough to be punished is good enough to be honoured; just as not every one who is not good enough to be honoured is bad enough to be punished.[112]

This essentially posits the doctrine of limbo before it had ever been suggested in the West. There is a third-place unbaptized infants must go because they have a sinful nature from Adam, but they have no personal sin. Indeed, on this point Gregory Nazianzen is actually closer to the greater Western tradition than even Augustine.

In commenting specifically upon Romans 5:12, St. John Chrysostom is clear that ἐφ' ᾧ refers to Adam, not death. "How then did death come in and prevail? 'Through the sin of one.' But what means, 'ἐφ' ᾧ πάντες ἥμαρτον?' This; he having once fallen, even they that had not eaten of the tree did from him, all of them, become

---

[111] Gregory Nazianzen, *Select Orations*, trans. Martha Vinson, (Washington: The Catholic University of America Press, 2003), 22.13.

[112] Gregory Nazianzen, *Select Orations of Saint Gregory Nazianzen*, in *Nicene and Post-Nicene Fathers, Second Series*, vol. 7., trans. Charles Gordon Browne and James Edward Swallow, ed. Philip Schaff and Henry Wace, (Buffalo, NY: Christian Literature Publishing Co., 1894), 40.23.

mortal."[113] All men, not just Adam, die because of the sin of Adam. Nowhere in this passage does Chrysostom even suggest that death is the cause of sin as the meaning of Romans 5:12. It is unclear whether Chrysostom takes it ἐφ here as "in" or "because."[114] This shows the closeness of these two ideas in the Greek Fathers. They did not try to separate these out into two concepts, but rather took it as one general idea of "ἐπί" for which there is no perfect English or Latin equivalent.

St. Cyril of Alexandria, who presided over the Council of Ephesus in which Pelagianism was condemned, also discusses the corporate personhood of Adam. While he does not interpret Romans 5:12 in this way, although he does hold that the relative refers to Adam, in many other spots Cyril does speak of mankind as in Adam.[115] At one point, Cyril says that God "struck us because of the transgression in Adam by saying, 'Earth you are, and to earth you will return [Gen 3:19].'"[116] All men receive a punishment, being stricken unto death, because of Adam. A punishment implies a guilt to merit receiving that punishment. Cyril follows the Cappadocians in the cause of corporate personhood, saying that "human nature was condemned in Adam."[117] Cyril denies a mere mimicry of Adam, clarifying that one does not die "because they sinned along with Adam, because they did not then exist, but because they had the same nature as Adam, which fell under the law of sin."[118] Meyendorff cites Cyril as his primary example against Augustine.[119] However, it is clear that Cyril is actually entirely in line with Augustine, not Meyendorff, in his account of sin.

Meyendorff's other main father that he uses against Augustine is St. Maximus the Confessor.[120] This is already a problematic line of argument because Maximus is two centuries after Augustine, so if

---

[113] John Chrysostom, *The Homilies of St. John Chrysostom, Archbishop of Constantinople, on the Epistle of St. Paul the Apostle to the Romans*, in *Nicene and Post-Nicene Fathers, First Series*, vol. 11, trans J. B. Morris and W. H. Simcox, rev. George B. Stevens, ed. Philip Schaff, (Buffalo, NY: Christian Literature Publishing Co., 1889), 10.1.

[114] Palmieri, 24-26.

[115] McCallum, 10-12.

[116] Cyril of Alexandria, *Commentary on John*, vol. 1, trans. David Maxwell, ed. Joel C. Elowsky, (Downers Grove: InterVarsity Press, 2013), 204.

[117] Cyril of Alexandria, *Commentary on John*, 694.

[118] Cyril, Explanation of the Letter to the Romans, PG 74 cols. 788–89, quoted in Gerald Bray, *Ancient Christian Commentary on Scripture: Romans*, (Downers Grove: Intervarsity Press, 2005).

[119] Meyendorff, 145.

[120] Meyendorff, 143-45.

there was discontinuity, it would be Maximus who is the innovator. However, there is once again continuity. While there is no direct proof that Maximus read Augustine, he spent much of his life in Carthage so Augustinian influence should not be surprising.[121] One of the key features that Meyendorff mentions is Maximus' view of the will. However, he holds the same view of the will as Augustine.[122] There is a natural will that reaches out towards the natural end of human nature, and another will which reaches out towards fallen desire. Maximus uses this other desire to develop the concept of the deliberative (γνωμικόν) will, while Augustine just calls this second desire concupiscence and leaves it at that. The two concepts are essentially the same in purpose. Meyendorff's insistence on calling it the "gnomic will" obscures its essential meaning, that it is a deliberation between choices. Even if one were to argue that Augustine does not develop his view far enough, this accusation cannot be placed on the larger western tradition as the scholastics actually adopted the distinction of the natural and deliberative wills from Maximus by way of St. John of Damascus.[123]

Maximus does not shy away from judicial language to speak of original sin. He calls death following from original sin a "natural debt."[124] He likewise speaks of how the whole of human nature is fallen in Adam, through whose "transgression sin gave subsistence to pleasure, and through pleasure affixed itself to the very foundations of our nature, condemning the whole of our nature to death."[125] He also speaks of this "just condemnation" as occurring "in Adam," which he contrasts with the redemption "in Christ."[126] The corporate personhood of Adam through human nature and the judicial language for original sin are both here. In many ways then, Maximus is actually the synthesis of the Eastern and Western traditions on original sin.

---

[121] Cooper, 89; Paul M. Blowers, *Maximus the Confessor: Jesus Christ and the Transfiguration of the World*, (Oxford: Oxford University Press, 2016), 28-31.

[122] von Balthasar, Hans Urs, *Cosmic Liturgy: The Universe According to Maximus the Confessor*, trans. Brian E. Daley, (San Francisco: Ignatius Press, 2003), 182-84.

[123] Tobias Hoffman, *Free Will and the Rebel Angels in Medieval Philosophy*, (Cambridge: Cambridge University Press, 2021), 23.

[124] Maximus the Confessor, *On Difficulties in Sacred Scripture in Response to Thalassios*, trans. Maximos Constas, (Washington: The Catholic University of America Press, 2018), 61.4.

[125] Maximus, 61.9.

[126] Maximus, 61.10.

VII. Conclusion

Taking together all this evidence, there does appear to be a unified theology of original sin in the Bible and the Fathers. All mankind was present in Adam at the fall through human nature. As a result, all infants are born with original guilt, although not personal guilt, which must be remitted by baptism if they are to enter Heaven. While it is a little unclear if "ἐφ'" in Romans 5:12 should be taken as "in" or "because," "ᾧ" certainly refers to Adam. Either interpretation of "ἐφ'" will lead to the same theology, and it seems this issue only exists in translation, not in Greek. What is important is the causal force of Adam's sin leading to death.

Almost none of Romanides' and Meyendorff's claims held up to scrutiny, which is not surprising given that barely any of Augustine's actual writings are cited by Romanides or Meyendorff. Romanides makes two brief citations to *De Gratia Christi de Peccato Originali* in one paragraph, but never cites him anywhere else.[127] Meyendorff briefly mentions Augustine's *De Trinitate*, but this work is not on original sin, and does not cite a single word of the actual work, so it does not appear he has actually read it.[128]

The claims of Romanides and Meyendorff do very closely mirror the claims of the Pelagians though. Both deny the force of original sin and the presence of humanity in Adam. Indeed, neither of them say anything negative about Pelagianism in their works. This leads one to believe that they were crypto-Pelagians. In their attempt to not be Latin, they have fallen into an error condemned by the East as well.

This shows the need to change the way apologetics and ecumenism are done. Romanides and Meyendorff came to the fathers with the preconceived notion that what the West believes must be wrong. This causes them to twist what is taught by both the East and West. Instead, one ought to be a serious scholar first and do apologetics or ecumenism only subordinated to it. There is nothing wrong with arguing one is correct or trying to reconcile the schism, but both of these must be done in truth because one ought to seek truth above all else. Indeed, in doing serious scholarship, it has been shown that the East and West actually are in agreement on original sin. When one places honesty and scholarship first, what follows can only be good if one is truly seeking the good and true.

---

[127] Romanides, 23.
[128] Meyendorff, 92, 190.

3

Saint Bonaventure and the Theology of Animals

Lance Gracy

In this essay I would like to provide a sort of metaphysical snapshot or portrait of St. Bonaventure's theology of animals. The intention, therefore, is to provide a framework in which an understanding of the gratuitous likeness or image of creatures can arise. In layman's terms, this gratuitous likeness or image refers to what subsists or is preserved in a creaturely being in the New Creation. As I would argue, for Bonaventure this gratuitous likeness or image is a *reformed substance* dependent upon its exemplar and made possible only through the prerogative of the divine will in accordance with the divine Art and the reward of glory. I will begin by identifying three interrelated concepts in the *Breviloquium*. I will then clarify some assumptions at the outset and proceed to examine each of Bonaventure's concepts in adequate detail. I conclude with relevant remarks.

I. Introduction

In his *Breviloquium*, Bonaventure puts forward a very intriguing statement on the status of plants and animals in the New Creation. He writes:

> Vegetative and sensitive beings do not possess the power of perpetual life and eternal duration that is reserved to the higher state, and so their whole substance will be consumed in fire. However, they will be preserved as ideas; and in a certain manner they will survive also in their likeness, humankind, who is kin to creatures of every species. And so one can say that *all things* will be *made new* and, in a certain sense, rewarded in the renovation and glorification of humanity.[1]

We should note that Bonaventure holds three concepts simultaneously with one another: (1) the lesser nobility of vegetative and sensitive beings (plants and animals) compared to rational beings; (2) despite this lesser nobility, a preservation and subsistence of these vegetative

---

[1] *Brev.*, 7.4.7.

and sensitive beings as "ideas" and, "in a certain manner," "also in their likeness," which is of humankind; and (3) that this partial continuation of animate species occurs with respect to the reward to be found in the "renovation and glorification of humanity." In what follows, I would like to extrapolate on these three interrelated concepts to elucidate how the subsistence or preservation of the idea and likeness of creatures—we will focus only on sensitive beings—is to be understood. But before proceeding to these concepts, we ought to make a few assumptions.

The first assumption is the reasonability of the following inference: sensitive beings are of an "institute for the purpose of signifying" which "not only has the character of sign in the ordinary sense of the term, but also the character of sacrament as well."[2] What this means generally is that all creatures speaking from the book of creation "tell us about *the uncreated Word.*"[3] The second assumption is that sensitive beings, while not made *naturally* in the image of God, could in theory be drawn up into a gratuitous image of God.[4] What we are interested in, therefore, is how specifically these assumptions ought to be understood, as well as *to what end* is our recognition of the truth of these assumptions. Before we examine them in the subsequent sections that deal with Bonaventure's three interrelated concepts, let us offer the following proposition to frame our inquiry: Although sensitive beings have neither understanding nor "eternity kept in memory," they nevertheless have a will that *could* subsist in the delight of such understanding and memory through relation to their exemplar.[5] Moreover, while it is the affective quality of the sensitive will, through its power of imagination that I think makes such a proposition intelligible, still, the sensitive will would need to, somehow, be elevated and configured into a reformed substance by

---

[2] *Itin.*, 2.12. Though there is gradation to the nobility of creatures, God chose every creature to signify His invisible qualities. At the highest grade are creatures which have been "raised by the Spirit of Prophecy to prefigure spiritual things in the book of Scriptures" and those which "it pleased God to appear through the ministry of the angels."

[3] *Comm. on Luke*, 18.59, p. 1783. Cf. Dan 3:57; Wis 13:5; Rom 1:20. The *triplex Verbum* concerns the uncreated, inspired, and incarnate Word. The inspired Word is that by which the first uncreated is pursued, and the incarnate is the resolving center of the two, the divine name of all Creation.

[4] This is the gloss of *Hex.*, 2.27.

[5] Ibid., *loc. cit.*

means of the rational creature and the divine Art, as the former possesses the required understanding and memory and the latter can "make it happen"; and that a reformed substance is necessary for the sensitive will to abide in the New Creation is shown in that, if the "whole substance" of the sensitive being (i.e., the body) is to be consumed, then, without a body, the animal would subsist *only* as a mere idea. But if the gratuitous image of the sensitive being is not a mere idea, it would need to include some superadded substantiality. As Bonaventure writes: "Since the soul will become supremely spiritual through the love of the highest Spirit, the body also must display a corresponding subtlety and spirituality."[6] In other words, if the sensitive being is to subsist (by its will), it seems there needs to be a corresponding image of the New Creation that is altogether different, or reformed, from its previous, natural image because, as Bonaventure states further: "God has a perpetual relation (*rationem*) with respect to the image of creation, of reparation, and of similitude; because the image is an essential dependency and relation (*relatio*)."[7] But let us move on to consider Bonaventure's three interrelated concepts, as these will help clarify the issue.

II. Species, Mode, and the Lesser Nobility of Sensitive Beings

For Bonaventure, a *species* is that by which the essence of a being is distinct from some other being, and it pertains to the "look" of a being.[8] We distinguish one species from another by the "essential look" a being has which differentiates it from whichever other. Understandably, then, we speak about the properties of a being when we refer to its species. The *mode* of a being, in contrast, is the manner by which or in which a particular species exercises its being. Here, too, we speak of a being's properties. Furthermore, the *order* of a being is that by which the species and mode are united together with respect to something else necessary for fulfilling the origin and completion of the essential being of a creature.[9] When Bonaventure refers to consummation of "the whole substance" of sensitive beings,

---

[6] *Brev.*, 7.7.4.

[7] *Hex.*, 10.7.

[8] Ibid., 2.24.

[9] Cf. *Hex.*, 10.7-15. Bonaventure has various general orders in which the fulfillment of a species occurs—e.g., demonstrations of the first universal Cause as invulnerable to an infinite regress, who is Being outside genus or beyond genus, and so forth.

I would venture to say he is referring to a change in the species by a new *order* of Being.[10] And yet, by "consumed," he is also referring to a *consummation* of the species, whereby a mode or manner of being is superadded to the species so to bring about a reformed substance, a completed essence, or a completed species.[11] That a being can receive a modification of the mode of being without that entailing an addition of essence is possible for Bonaventure because of the *ratio seminalis*, or the radical root potential. According to this notion, a species can receive a *completed* essence because the radical root potential of a being is itself an active potency joined to a passive potency while the active and passive parts are yet founded upon different principles in a being.[12] In its natural state, the sensitive being exercises one side of the intermediate form of potency, the active potency; and as a sensitive being that has yet to receive a modification of the mode of being, or has yet to receive its completed species, it retains the other side of the intermediate form of potency, a passive but not merely passive potency.[13] Metaphysically, then, an animal could receive a modification to its mode of being that would complete its species while not nullifying its nature or some aspect of its nature. As the maxim goes: *Gratia non tollit naturam sed perficit.*

Now to assess the dilemma: To be capable of blessedness, a soul has to be immortal; but if the soul is the form of the body, it follows "that the soul is united to a mortal body in such a manner that it can be separated from it"[14] because an immortal soul would need to be joined to an incorruptible body. By what exemplary form could an animal soul be joined to an incorruptible body? While both the human and animal have a separable soul, they differ in the act of conformity of body and spirit. To know what a creature is universally,[15] is to know what the creature is in its bodily form, especially as the body is consubstantial with an unfulfilled and yet intelligible potency

---

[10] I.e., Since the futility of a created cause cannot fully account for the nobility of the species, the change wrought in a species is by the order of origin in the divine Art, which may be regarded as a gain of life or material expression from less noble to more noble in the Divine 'to Be.'

[11] Or even, perhaps, a "pure vestige."

[12] *Hex.*, 4.10.

[13] Ibid., *loc. cit.*

[14] *Brev.*, 2.9.5.

[15] At least in the sense that the universal is in the soul. Generally, Bonaventure holds that the universal is partly in the soul and partly in God.

conveyed by the activity of that creature according to whichever genus or kind it belongs to. The human creature specifically has this universal being *in substantia, in corporeitate, in animalitate.*[16] Animals are not in this universal being *in corporeitate*, nor, naturally, *in substantia.* They participate *in animalitate*, but, again, if the soul is the form of the body, the animal's participation in the genus of humanity cannot be absolute. However, I think the animal's participation can be eschatologically meaningful. Consider, for instance, that the common nature of the sensitive and rational soul has two distinct principles operating within it, as expressed above in our overview of potency. According to Bonaventure's doctrine of *unibilitas*, or the twofold manner in which the soul is united to the body, "[T]he soul is united to the body not only as a perfection, but also as a mover; its essence perfects what it likewise directs."[17] As a perfecting power, the soul is united to human being in a way that differs essentially from animals. As a moving power, however, the soul of humans and animals is united to each respective body in a common manner. As the soul directs the rational soul, it does so according to the special operations of the rational soul; as it directs the sensitive soul, it does so according to the special operations of the sensitive soul. But the question becomes whether the sensitive soul, as only sensitive and not as rational, can be directed towards divine being. The rational soul is directed toward divine being out of intellect or understanding, but what about the sensitive soul? To illustrate: what was it that moved Balaam's donkey?[18] Was the donkey's affective will not inspired by the Angel before it or by some devout aspect of its nature that showed allegiance to his handler? Tentatively, it seems more than possible for the sensitive soul to be directed, by means of some imaginative will, to the divine image.

At any rate, let us offer some theological and metaphysical ground to the aforementioned: If the end imposes a necessity on those things that pertain to the end,[19] and if the end of sensitive beings is in a gratuitous image through which their substance is in some way

---

[16] Cf. the Delorme translation of *Hex.*, 4.9.

[17] *Brev.*, 2.9.5. Cf. Aristotle, *On Generation and Corruption*, 1.39.5. Also see Thomas Osborne, "*Unibilitas* : The Key to Bonaventure's Understanding of Human Nature," in *Journal of the History of Philosophy*, 37:2 (1999): 227-250.

[18] Cf. Num 22:22-39.

[19] Bonaventure derives this from Aristotle, *Physics*, 2.9. Cf. *Brev.*, 2.9.4.

glorified by grace, it is necessary that there be an exemplar by which any being can be noble despite their relative ignobility. Framed another way, if all creation is subject to an "essential relation" or "essential passion" to God, as Bonaventure maintains,[20] then there ought to be a highest Spirit in which any creature can receive an act that perfects its being. Let us consider this in terms of the "idea and likeness" of creatures.

III. The Idea and Likeness of Creatures

"[E]very creature is by its very nature a figure and likeness of eternal Wisdom…"[21] The figure and likeness of eternal Wisdom, which is expressive of the unfulfilled, devout aspect or potency of creatures, can be regarded as *an exemplary cause* on the supposition that the creature stretches out toward the Truth Itself, or God, in which its similitude is most highly expressed.[22] The exemplary likeness of the creature, then, is an image and imitation by way of expression[23] and the reason for its being is held in the acuity of the Word, which understands "whatever is and whatever can be," and by having the exemplars of things within itself, equates the reason of understanding (*ratio intelligendi*) with the understanding (*intellectus*) of the highest Spirit as a similitude or likeness.[24] Therefore, in a sense, the higher expression or image of the sensible creature in the Word supersedes the base nature of the creature because more than the sensible creature is a nature, it is "a way leading to the Exemplar,"[25] and the more primary a thing is with respect to its end, the more it supersedes less-primary things that pertain thereto. In other words, what is more primary about a creature than its nature is its *vestige*, a footprint of the divine essence, "a certain representation (*simulacrum*) of the wisdom

---

[20] *Hex.*, 4.8.

[21] *Itin.*, 2.12.

[22] *I Sent.*, 35.1, resp.

[23] Cf. Leonard Bowman, "The Cosmic Exemplarism of Bonaventure," in *The Journal of Religion*, 55:2 (1975): 181-198. Bowman writes: "Within this doctrine of relations of expression, the exemplar is the active side of expression: that which expresses itself. Its correlative, the passive expression or that in which the exemplar is expressed, is called an image."

[24] *Hex.*, 3.4.

[25] Ibid., 12.14.

of God."[26] In the relation of exemplarity, or in the relation of vestige to uncreated Word, a creature possesses a dignity unlike any other. For instance, as Bonaventure says, "Although an Angel shares more with the Word in its noble condition, as a pure image of God, than does a worm; nevertheless, in the relation (*ratione*) of exemplarity, the relation (*ratio*) of an Angel is not nobler than a worm."[27] In other words, the Word expresses the likeness or idea of a creature better than any other creature could because, for one, it has the species described within itself and brings the species "to be"[28]; and for another, the Word expresses the idea of the creature through an immediate, intrinsic act of *creating* rather than by a mediate, extrinsic act of *created.*[29] In this way, God "presides over the direction of all acts insofar as they are governable; not like an artisan who abandons the house once it is made; instead God conserves and directs all things."[30] Taken together with Bonaventure's argument that perfect unity does not exist in creatures but only in God,[31] the view that God presides over the direction of creatures and establishes norms for the creature should be taken to mean that only God, not nature, can express and order the creature's ultimate end. This truth of creatures in the highest was missed by the philosophers who knew only the nature of things in themselves, but not those things as vestige.[32] It is missed by anyone who does not belong to "the highest of contemplatives," of which St. Francis is the exemplary model,[33] and those lacking in monastic and moral discipline and metaphysical preparation. All the same, "Both reason (*ratio*) and faith lead to these exemplary splendors (*splendores exemplares*)."[34]

IV. On the Essential Relation of the Sensitive, Rational, and Divine

The essential relation of sensitive and rational creatures to God is

---

[26] Ibid., *loc. cit.*

[27] Ibid., 3.8.

[28] Ibid., 12.8, 13.

[29] Ibid., 12.10.

[30] Ibid., 12.4.

[31] Ibid., 11.8.

[32] Ibid., 12.15.

[33] Ibid., *loc. cit.*

[34] Ibid., 12.14.

either according to a natural or gratuitous image. In the rational soul, this natural image is of memory, understanding (*intelligentia*), and will, "in which the Trinity shines forth (*relucet*)."[35] As for the gratuitous image, which is either the rational soul reformed by grace or the Intelligences, this is a *sealed* image of memory in eternity, understanding in wisdom, and the will in enjoyment of "goodness that delights in the will,"[36] The crux of our inquiry arises here: Can there in any way be such a thing as a gratuitous image of the sensitive soul? If so, what could be the *seal* of such?

I have been suggesting in one part of this article or another that the sensitive will is of a nature that it could rightfully be transferred to a sealed image of enjoyment in goodness and delight.[37] Supposing that all three—i.e., memory, understanding, and will—are necessary for an individual soul to subsist in the New Creation, how could a creature in principle having only one of these three possibly exist in it? If, as Bonaventure says, only the substantial human soul is "disposed towards resurrection in the order of necessity,"[38] what could be spoken of in truth about God gathering the animal soul into a substantial form? I think an essential order between sensitive, rational, and divine is present in divine Wisdom in a twofold, mutually reinforcing way: (1) by the love or the affection of the intelligence animating the sensitive soul towards the gratuitous image,[39] and (2) by the divine Art

---

[35] Ibid., 2.27.

[36] Ibid., *loc. cit.*

[37] I do not find this explicitly in Bonaventure's works but I see no reason to deny it. After all, if non-human animals are vestiges of divine wisdom, they must carry—however latently that may be—some *redeemable power* of divine wisdom. It is not in the intellect because, even if animals have intelligence, this is not what we mean by "understanding," and it is not in blessed memory because animals do not have understanding. Furthermore, if it is *in corporeitate*, it is so only metaphorically. And if *in substantia*, it is so only hypothetically. But the will brings together affection, some semblance of intelligence, and related things.

[38] *Rrov.*, 7.5.5.

[39] This is a rather standard approach to resolving theological questions concerning animals—their consciousness, status, possible existence in heaven, etc.—but without some existing prerogative, I think it is difficult to maintain without devolving into sentimentalism. Nevertheless, there are many examples one could choose from here: e.g., the story of Balaam's donkey; Noah's ark; the animals that tended to the Christ Child, who, as Bonaventure notes, were moved by love "as if" by reason; or in various other illustrations of the saints, such as those of St. Francis, St. Anthony of Padua, St. Joseph Cupertino, St. Margaret of Cortona, St. Roch of Montpellier, St. Don Bosco, and others.

necessitating a First Cause that is not by nature, but by a noble mode of emanation.[40] These two can be unified the cognition of divine Wisdom through the highest Spirit of binding love. As Bonaventure says: "Wisdom…consists in cognition (*cognitione*); and where there is cognition (*cognitio*), it is necessary that there would be an emanation or generation of a word; from that generation there follows the production of binding love (*amoris nectentis*)."[41] Thus, the "production of binding love" is a terminus of sorts: a bond of matter and form at the summit of affective union living in the everlasting forms of the divine will. Thus, in the generation of the uncreated Word is present the divine plan of the incarnate Word, and by the emanational wisdom of the inspiring Word, a sensitive will receives the production of binding love given freely from the incarnate love of the Son, who dignified the matter of rational creatures in His nature. Let us consider this in more depth.

In the resurrection, "all shall come forth, whole and perfect, *into a perfect man, into the measure of the age of the fullness of Christ.*"[42] Since nature was subjected to futility,[43] this resurrection cannot be brought about by seminal or natural causes; it can only be brought about by the divine First Cause.[44] As Bonaventure says: "The creature comes forth from the Creator, but not through nature, because God is of another nature; therefore it is by art, since there is no other noble mode of emanating than by nature or by art, that is, from will."[45] In the context of origin and resurrection, if it is necessary for an immortal soul to have an immortal body,[46] the adjacent principle for the sensitive soul seems necessary too—namely, that, for the exemplary splendor of a sensitive soul to be made manifest, a restoration of the original intent in the Divine Exemplar, in cooperation with the divine plan of Creation, ought to permit some glorification through grace. Although this need not include the whole of what is from nature, still, if whatever is from nature agrees with art, it can be permitted. I submit that the will of sensitive souls can agree with divine Art—not in that

---

[40] *Hex.*, 12.3.

[41] Ibid., 11.4.

[42] *Brev.*, 7.5.4.

[43] Cf. Rom 8:20.

[44] *Brev.*, 7.5.5.

[45] *Hex.*, 12.3.

[46] *Brev.*, 7.5.5.

the sensitive soul, by its own power of representation or of "imaging," agrees fully, but rather in the sense that what is signified in the sensitive power is conducive to either *prophetic prefigurement, angelic operation*, or *supernatural institution*, as Bonaventure himself suggests.[47] Thus, the divine Art, by impressing contingent things with infallible expressions of exemplarity, can conserve or preserve contingent things in such a way that the creature represents the spiritual and everlasting and "lives in eternal forms."[48] If the divine Art restores creation in this exemplary fashion, does this happen automatically as though it merely followed rationally from agreement between nature and art?

God, the Divine Artist, can fashion sensitive souls into a reformed substance or "new image" for the sake of pleasing the understanding, memory, and will of the nobler creatures, who have turned toward the "contuiting (*contuendo*) of divine spectacles (*spectacula*)" and toward "tasting divine consolations."[49] Thus, in the contuition of divine love between virtue and vestige, a righteous soul could recognize the prerogative of the Divine Artist to satisfy mystical wisdom, which is "above every substance and knowledge,"[50] and to establish a bond or complement at the end of knowledge's formal certitude. The soul's ascent 'to be' in this way could also be understood as an ascent to reward on behalf of the treasure and glory of heaven. I see no reason to deny that the will of animals could be elevated and conjoined to a gratuitous image insofar as there is a rational soul present to receive it as a gift, to understand, enjoy, and recall its significance. Importantly, though, what makes the animal a worthy candidate for all this is not up to the arbitrary will of the human creature, but to the prerogative of the divine will in the divine Art. And since Christ, the image of the invisible God and one propitiation for sin, was resurrected into a new body, why not those creatures which prefigured Him in the Temple sacrifice? Since Christ glorified, the divine image of the New Creation, was ministered to by Angels, why not those creatures which similarly tended to Him? Since Christ instituted the sacraments of the Church for the glorification and renovation of the whole world, did He not also institute it for the glorification and renovation of every

---

[47] *Itin.*, 2.12.

[48] *Hex.*, 12.7, 13. The quote comes from Augustine.

[49] Ibid., 5.24.

[50] Ibid., 2.29.

creature of the world? We can in some manner answer in the affirmative to each of these questions. I would conclude, then, that our inquiry has led us to say sensitive beings carry an aspect, trace, or seminal reason of this divine prerogative in their will—an unfulfilled potency of the will and imagination capable of being joined to an exemplary splendor and form through a production of highest spiritual love.

V. Conclusion

A reformed soul healed by grace recognizes that it "ought to pass over (*transire*) from the shadow to the light (*lucem*), from the way to the end, from the vestige to the truth, from the book to true knowledge (*scientam*), which is in God."[51] We have, I am sure, heard many sentiments about deceased animals: "Fido is in heaven." "Fido has crossed over the rainbow bridge." I think there is some truth to these sentiments insofar as they indicate a faithful, trusting, and loving virtue[52]; but sadly, they fall short of the "metaphysical backbone" of a theology of animals. Other than a common aspect of *will* in whichever respective genus or kind of animal, the animal one would see in heaven by the good pleasure of God will hardly be recognizable— though, for all that, the vision will be far more joyous than any earthly vision. But what about the substantial reality of the being? What about the gratuitous image? Falling upon the insight of Maimonides, we could say this "comes in a dream or in a vision"[53] insofar as the destiny of sensitive souls is a true reality by way of prophetic prefigurement. Otherwise, I suspect the soul could only concoct its imaginations under an eternal type of repose. But if I may, I would like to offer an anecdote:

Not long ago, I had a dream. In the dream, I felt as though I were entering a final repose. I walked into a small house in the middle of a large field and was greeted by loved ones. It felt like a celebration, like some ethereal wedding feast of sorts. The euphoria was palpable. I looked across the room and saw my grandmother, who passed away while I was in Afghanistan. I looked along the wall and saw another creature, and I fed myself on the sight of this otherworldly creature.

---

[51] *Hex.*, 12.15.

[52] Ibid., 7.18.

[53] *Guide* 2.36 78b.

As I gazed in awe at it, I felt a great cloud of witnesses looking upon me, rejoicing in my vision, which felt like a reward greater than anything I had ever before received. As I looked at the creature and felt the adulation of my onlookers, a beloved pet came to mind I had known long ago—one of whom I had blessed on the feast day of St. Francis. I can recall now how God had formerly summoned my mind to wisdom by bathing that pet of mine in an aura as I prayed the Rosary for the first time; how he placed his paw on my lap and looked at me with doleful eyes as I was living alone and adjusting to civilian life after a terrible divorce and military service; how grieved I was when he passed away and felt his life departing; and how acute the pain was that I felt at his loss upon arriving home that evening to my wife and newborn daughter. The memory was a special one, a sacred one. But in the dream, there was neither sorrow nor sentiment. Before me was only a new creation. The form and appearance of the creature that had caused me pain was not there. What I saw was something entirely new. It was like a wisp, a ghost, a mass of spiritual matter in cosmic celebration. As I reached forward to touch this creature, my hands suddenly extended throughout its matter as if there were no end to it. This gift, this reward, felt to me like angelic dough, a rich and endless depth as white as snow and as translucent as a ghost. Words hardly do justice.

How can perfect wisdom, a wisdom *hidden in mystery*, be comprehended if it has not *entered into the human heart* or is not yet without form? The preparation of the soul to this point is such that its comprehension of various forms informs the final status of truth and wisdom, the summit of the excess of love, just in the way the head informs the heart by adding to it richness and adornment. The treasures of the heart are revealed by God, but the light of the understanding illumines these treasures. But the Seraphic Doctor, quoting the Magnificent Doctor, should have the final word:

> But how great these goods are, and how manifold, I shall state, not in my own words, but in those of blessed Anselm, who writes towards the end of his *Proslogion*: "Now, my soul, rouse yourself and lift up your whole understanding; think as much as you can on what kind and how great this good is. For if particular goods are enjoyable, consider carefully how enjoyable is that Good which contains the joyfulness of all goods. This is not a joy such as we have experienced in created things, but as different from this as the Creator is from the creature. For if life that is created is good, how good is the Life that creates? If the salvation that has been wrought is joyful, how joyful is the Salvation that brings about all

salvation? If wisdom in the knowledge of things that have been brought into being is loveable, how loveable is the Wisdom that has brought all things into being from nothing? Finally, if there are many delights in delightful things, of what kind and how great is the delight in the One who made these same delightful things?"[54]

[54] *Brev.*, 7.7.6.

Part II: Catholic Social Teaching and the Theology of Creation

4

True and False Creation: Contextualizing the Theology of *Laudato si'*

Gideon Lazar

A constant source of heresies within the Church has been false teachings about creation. This is because the act of creation reveals something about the creator God. Therefore, those who seek to teach false things about God frequently do so by either denying or distorting his creative work. However, God has provided a polemic to put to rest all false teachings about creation: He has revealed the creation of the world itself to us.

An early example of the use of Genesis this way is by St. John Chrysostom. He argues that,

> When a Manichean tells you that the matter pre-existed, and when Marcion, Valentine, or a Gentile support you the same opinion, answer them that in the beginning God created heaven and earth; but if they reject the authority of Scripture, treat them as extravagant and foolish.[1]

We ought not to listen to the wisdom of the world on creation, as it often serves as a source of error. Chrysostom continues,

> Have men taught me what I am about to reveal to you? By no means, but He alone who has worked these wonders, leads and directs my tongue to teach them to you: I conjure you therefore to impose silence on all human reasoning, and not to listen to this narrative as if it were not as the word of Moses. For it is God himself who speaks to us, and Moses is only his interpreter. The reasoning of man, says the Scripture, is timid, and his thoughts uncertain. (Wis 9:14) Let us, then, accept the divine word with humble deference, without exceeding the limits of our intelligence, nor curiously seeking what it cannot attain. But the enemies of the truth do not know these rules, and they want to appreciate all the works of the Lord according to the only lights of reason. Insane! They forget that the mind of man is too narrow to probe these mysteries.[2]

---

[1] John Chrysostom, *Homilies on Genesis 1-17,* trans. Robert C. Hill, (Washington, D.C.: The Catholic University of America Press, 1986), 2.3.

[2] Chrysostom, 2.2.

I. Genesis in its Ancient Near Eastern Context

Chrysostom's approach is not something entirely new in his day. Indeed, many modern scholars have argued that even in its original context, the creation story served as a counternarrative to various pagan myths the Israelites would have been familiar with.

Genesis opens with the radical claim that "In the beginning, God created the heavens and the Earth" (Gen 1:1). This contrasts with the claims of almost all ancient pagan religions that the world was made out of preexistent matter. In the Mesopotamian *Enuma Elish*, the world originates as a primordial war between Tiamat and the gods. In Egyptian creation myths, the world comes about through a sort of emanation of divinity from a primordial ocean. Some Egyptian accounts, such as the earliest at Heliopolis, the first god performs sexually immoral acts on himself to create. In all these accounts, there is not a creation *ex nihilo*, but an ordering of what already existed. This ordering is frequently done through gravely sinful means. Genesis denies all of that. It says that God simply created. The ordering only happens after God has already created formless matter. In the shaping of this formless matter, God does not need to use sinful means. He does not have to fight an equal. He does not have to perform sexual acts. He simply creates and orders all things as He wishes.

In addition, in the many pagan creation myths, such as the Egyptian ones, the different things in the universe are gods. Thus, creation itself becomes personified and deified. Genesis strikes down such a view. Everything is made of matter, not pagan gods, and even that matter was made by God. Thus, creation is something distinct from the divine, not to be worshiped, but also came from the divine, and thus worship of that God is still necessary. Genesis thereby rejects both idolatry and paganism.

When it comes to the creation of man, the Mesopotamians had an especially brutal account. According to the *Atra-hasis*, man was created because the gods got tired and needed slaves to do their work for them. While man is created to do work in Genesis, he was created in the image of God, not as a slave, to continue the creative work of God. Thus, man's labor is not servile work but is dignified.[3]

Likewise, God does not rest because He is tired, as in the Atra-

---

[3] John Paul II, *Laborem exercens*.

hasis. As Isaiah says, "The Lord is the everlasting God, the Creator of the ends of the earth. He does not faint or grow weary" (Isa 40:28). Rather, God enters into a rest of worship. He does this to establish a pattern for man to follow. Man works and then enters into rest, just as God did. This sabbath rest is the purpose of man's work. This contrasts with the pagan vision where rest granted to a worker was only so that they could be a better worker the next day when they continued working. In Egyptian society for example, living slaves would be entombed with Pharaohs so that they could continue to serve their master in the next life. Slaves never enter into true rest and worship of God in paganism. They do according to Genesis, however.

Erroneous understandings of God, nature, and man all come about when one has a wrong understanding of creation. Genesis serves not just as a polemic in the sense of just being a direct condemnation, but rather it worked as a condemnation by unveiling the true order of creation. Thus, it serves not just a polemic in its original context but can be used as a source against new errors as they arise. The Church successfully refuted many false conceptions of the world through the creation story revealed in scripture. Thus, in order to overturn Christendom, a new creation story would be needed for the liberal order.

II. The Creation Myth of Liberalism

One of the key founders of our modern world is Thomas Hobbes. Living in the 17th century, Hobbes saw the endless violence of his own day and wished to propose a solution. In his book *Leviathan*, Hobbes envisions how governments began to exist in the first place. Having already articulated a specifically anti-scholastic theory of politics in the first twelve chapters, in chapter 13 Hobbes explains the original state of man. Since, for the most part, "Nature hath made men so equal in the faculties of body and mind" and subject to the passions of "fear of death; desire of such things as are necessary to commodious living; and a hope by their industry to obtain them," man is naturally in a state of "war of every man against every man" in which "nothing can be unjust. The notions of right and wrong, justice and injustice, have there no place." Man is naturally ruled by his passions which leads to endless conflict with his neighbor.

This leads Hobbes in the next chapter to articulate his vision of the natural law. Hobbes brings up the issue of the distinction between *jus* (right) and *lex* (law). He understands this distinction as that "right consisteth in liberty to do, or to forbear; whereas law determineth and bindeth to one of them: so that law and right differ as much as obligation and liberty." This means that the natural law and natural right, traditionally understood as two aspects of the same thing, are now opposed to one another. Hobbes defines natural right as the freedom to do what one wishes, while the natural law is the desire to preserve one's own life. Therefore, men have to come out of the state of nature, the war of all against all, and abandon this natural right of absolute freedom to the state, which receives its power from the social contract. At this point, the sovereign of the state is free to create whatever laws he wishes, because that is necessary to preserve the peace.

There are certainly elements of truth within Hobbes's narrative. For example, it is the case that men are by nature relatively equal, as all men are made in the image of God. Likewise, it is the case that men at certain times come together to form governments. However, the central error of Hobbes is, as many contemporary critics pointed out, that his supposed state of nature never happened.[4] His views sound more like the pagan myths, such as the similarities with ancient near eastern myths that the Israelites knew of, or like the Greco-Roman myths his contemporary critics were familiar with, such as those found in Horace and Lucretius. However, scripture reveals that man was created in a garden with pre-existing social relationships, and even after the fall we see man as farmers, shepherds, and city builders within the first generations of humans. Genesis reveals that man is by nature a political being.

The errors of Hobbes can be seen clearly by comparing him with his near contemporary, Fr. Francisco Suarez, SJ. Suarez was very well known even in the Protestant world and Hobbes was undoubtedly familiar with his work. In book three of *De Legibus*, Suarez conducts a similar thought experiment to Hobbes on how governments form.[5] However, the answers Suarez comes to are very different. Suarez points out how man was created and is by nature a political animal. Man has always existed in relationships and therefore needs to be

---

[4] Pat Moloney, "Leaving the Garden of Eden: Linguistic and Political Authority in Thomas Hobbes," *History of Political Thought* 18, no. 2 (1997): 249-254.

[5] A translation of this the relevant chapters of *De Legibus* can be found in Francisco Suarez, *Selections from Three Works*, trans. Gwladys L. Williams, Ammi Brown, and John Waldron, (Indianapolis: Liberty Fund, 2015).

directed to the common good. Even before the fall then, mankind would have needed a political authority as we grew from a single couple into a larger community. While the fall means that there must now be a coercive aspect to law, it still would have been directive apart from the fall. As an additional proof, Suarez points out how even the angels exist within a natural hierarchy. While it is true that at times civilization falls into disorder, since man is naturally political, we come together to form a community and we freely give political authority into the hands of a group or individual to help guide society.

This is the key difference between Hobbes and Suarez. Suarez starts with man as revealed in scripture. The state of nature is man in the garden, man in community. Sin corrupts, but does not destroy, human nature. For Hobbes, the state of nature is a state of chaos out of which we must ascend. Hobbes therefore has to reject the Eden story and come up with a new creation myth. While Hobbes does discuss Adam a number of times in *Leviathan*, Adam oddly does not come up in the discussion of how man originally was, the spot where it would be most important to mention him.

This difference can again be seen in how Hobbes departs from the classical understanding of the natural law. The natural law is no longer about conforming oneself to nature so that one can best perfect his own human nature, but it becomes about violence. Right is no longer the object of justice which arises from the natural law, but rather is something unrelated to justice and opposed to law. While this could sound like unimportant philosophical nuances, it is not. This is nothing short of a rejection of the entire tradition of Catholic moral theology, and Hobbes was intentionally doing this.

Hobbes's rejection of natural law leads him to think that man is naturally ruled by the lower passions of desire and fear because of the natural scarcity of the world. However, Marc Barnes has pointed out how this fundamental assumption of liberalism is contrary to how the Church Fathers interpreted Genesis.[6] They saw man as starting out in a state of abundance in the garden, and scarcity, leading to the rule of the lower passions, only comes about because of sin.

How did this origin come about? Barnes argues it was the

---

[6] Marc Barnes, "Adam without Scarcity," New Polity, 2019. https://newpolity.com/blog/malthus. Barnes, "What Becomes of Eden When Adam Becomes Afraid," New Polity, 2019. https://newpolity.com/blog/adam-afraid.

discovery of the Americas.[7] The discovery of a whole new group of peoples without any apparent civilization led to a new vision of the origins of civilization. Rather than hunter-gathering being seen as a degeneration of society, as men were originally gardeners and farmers, this tribal way of life was seen as where all civilization came from. This vision of civilization thus became ingrained in the imagination of the West ever since.

III. Pope Francis's Critique of Liberalism

When the Popes began to teach on issues of social teaching they consistently returned to Genesis as the source of these teachings. Pope Leo XIII makes this very clear when defending the dignity of marriage against the beginnings of the modern sexual revolution.

> The true origin of marriage, venerable brothers, is well known to all. Though revilers of the Christian faith refuse to acknowledge the never-interrupted doctrine of the Church on this subject, and have long striven to destroy the testimony of all nations and of all times, they have nevertheless failed not only to quench the powerful light of truth, but even to lessen it. We record what is to all known, and cannot be doubted by any, that God, on the sixth day of creation, having made man from the slime of the earth, and having breathed into his face the breath of life, gave him a companion, whom He miraculously took from the side of Adam when he was locked in sleep. God thus, in His most far-reaching foresight, decreed that this husband and wife should be the natural beginning of the human race, from whom it might be propagated and preserved by an unfailing fruitfulness throughout all futurity of time.[8]

In *Veritatis splendor*, Pope St. John Paul II points out that this follows the pattern of Our Lord, who turned to Genesis when responding to the Pharisees for divorce, the social issue of His day (c.f. Mark 10:6-9). While all of sacred scripture is important for moral theology, St. John Paul II points out that Genesis is especially important because it reveals the patterns of the created order, and so it sheds an important light on natural law.

St. John Paul II himself invoked creation many times in his pontificate, such as to defend the dignity of marriage in *Theology of the Body*, or to defend the dignity of labor in *Laborem exercens*. One

---

[7] Marc Barnes and Jacob Imam, "Adam Without Liberalism," New Polity, podcast audio, 2020. https://newpolity.com/podcasts-hub/adam-without-liberalism.
[8] Leo XIII, *Arcanum divinae* 5.

of the clearest invocations though has been in our own day by Pope Francis.

This give us the proper context for considering the papal encyclical *Laudato si'*. In it, Pope Francis lays out a devastating critique of the excesses of modern society and the effects of this on the environment. While the encyclical has often been considered as an element of the wider secular environmentalist movement, this is the wrong setting for it. Rather, the encyclical is grounded within the Catholic theologies of creation and of politics. If taken seriously, the encyclical can be taken as a deathblow to the contemporary materialist understanding of the cosmos and to the politics of secular liberalism.

In chapter two of *Laudato Si'*, the Holy Father lays out the theology of creation. The section begins by explaining how God created man with three different relations: "with God, with our neighbour and with the earth itself".[9] We see this in Genesis 2. God speaks to man, man speaks to woman, and man speaks to the animals. However, we also see that these three relationships are not equal. There is a Dionysian hierarchy of goods, with God as the highest good, and then going down through the angels, man, and all of creation. Francis stresses this hierarchy of goods in many places. For example, he calls on us "to praise God the Creator" and complains of those who "combat trafficking in endangered species while remaining completely indifferent to human trafficking, unconcerned about the poor, or undertaking to destroy another human being deemed unwanted."[10]

This is not to say that care for creation is unimportant. After all, this is exactly what the encyclical is about. Francis refers to creation as a "common good" as it is something we can all share in.[11] Likewise, Francis draws on the concept of *exitus* and *reditus* when he argues that just as God created all things, these creatures "give glory to God by their very existence" and "convey their message to us."[12] God's *ad extra* work goes down through the great chain of being which then returns that gift of love back through the chain to God. In terms of our relations with animals, this means we have a duty to care for them and in return they serve us in a variety of ways.

---

[9] *Laudato si'* (hereafter *LS*) 66.
[10] *LS* 72, 91.
[11] *LS* 23
[12] *LS* 33.

Francis points out how "these three vital relationships have been broken, both outwardly and within us. This rupture is sin. The harmony between the Creator, humanity and creation as a whole was disrupted."[13] Man is in the middle of the great chain of being, and so God set up man as a priest in the garden to mediate His life to the creation. The words to till (*abad*) and to keep (*shamar*) in the original Hebrew are actually the same words used for the priests in the temple.[14] If we follow through the seven days of creation, we find they actually match up perfectly with the seven speeches that God gives to Moses in creating the Tabernacle in Exodus and again the seven steps that Moses uses to actually build the Tabernacle.[15] We see when Solomon builds the temple he spends six years building the Temple and on the seventh year he consecrates the temple (1 Kings 6:38). We also find that if we lay out the structure of the garden and compare that to the structure of the Tabernacle in Exodus, they match up perfectly.[16] The Garden in Eden is a temple in which man mediates God's life to creation by serving as the priest.

Sin destroys this connection. Sin not only destroys relations between man and his neighbor and between man and God, but also between man and creation because it ruptures this chain of being. For example, when Cain kills Abel, God tells Cain that,

> The voice of your brother's blood is crying to me from the ground. And now you are cursed from the ground, which has opened its mouth to receive your brother's blood from your hand. When you till the ground, it shall no longer yield to you its strength (Gen 4:10-12).[17]

The effects of Cain's sin seep down into the very fabric of creation and this has a very real effect on Cain's agricultural production. Sin continues on the Earth regardless though, and eventually the world becomes so filled with violence that "all the fountains of the great deep

---

[13] *LS* 66.

[14] G. K. Beale, *The Temple and God's Mission: A Biblical Theology of the Dwelling Place of God*, (Downers Grove: InterVarsity Press, 2004), 66-77.

[15] Ratzinger, *The Spirit of the Liturgy*, trans. John Saward, (San Francisco: Ignatius Press, 2000), 26-27; Peter J. Kearney, "Creation and Liturgy: The P Redaction of Ex 25—40," *Zeitschrift für die alttestamentliche Wissenschaft* 89, no. 3 (1977): 375-387.

[16] For a detailed study of the development of temple imagery in scripture, see Jordan, *Through New Eyes: Developing a Biblical View of the World*, (Brentwood: Wolgemuth & Hyatt, Publishers, Inc., 1988) and Stephen Smith, *The House of the Lord: A Catholic Biblical Theology of God's Temple Presence in the Old and New Testaments*, (Steubenville: Franciscan University Press, 2007).

[17] C.f. *LS* 70.

burst forth and the windows of the heavens were opened" (Gen 7:11).[18] The Earth itself comes forth to prosecute the violence against it.

All of this may sound like nice allegories to learn about the relationship between man and creation. However, the Holy Father is clear that "the creation accounts in the book of Genesis contain… historical reality."[19] He does clarify that it is in "symbolic language." After all, there are not really windows in the sky or fountains under the ground. However, these are real stories that really happened. To reduce them to allegory would be to turn Christianity into a Gnostic religion where the creation does not matter. Our sins and salvation history take place in this world, not some disembodied world of ideas. This is the very theme of *Laudato si'* after all. Thus, the stories told in Genesis must be real stories that actually happened or else the very message of the encyclical risks falling apart.

The Holy Father's message also strikes a blow at the secular materialist account of the cosmos. According to this view it is not sin that damages creation. Sin, if it exists at all, is a matter for the disembodied world of philosophy and religion. It has no impact upon natural processes. What is damaging creation is specific technologies that are producing specific effects. This is partially correct. We are using certain technologies that are damaging the environment. However, these technologies are part of a wider sinful regime of technocracy, as Francis points out.[20] It is the sinful system that is destroying the world. Environmentally destructive technology is merely the secondary cause by which technocracy destroys. In the time of Cain, his sin still had an effect on the environment. Indeed, it led to the near extinction of all life during the flood. Thus, sin's destruction of the cosmos is a perennial issue which has now simply taken a new form which Pope Francis thinks requires new tools to combat.

Going back even further than Cain, St. Paul says that "the creation was subjected to futility, not of its own will but by the will of him who subjected it in hope; because the creation itself will be set free from its bondage to decay and obtain the glorious liberty of the children of

---

[18] C.f. *LS* 70.
[19] *LS* 66.
[20] *LS* 101-136.

God" (Rom 8:20-21).[21] Adam was set as the head of creation, and so in a sense his sin disordered not only the human family, but also the whole cosmos.[22]

Since the cause of environmental destruction is twofold, both human sin and particular actions of technologies, a twofold solution is needed. To the problem of human sin, the Holy Father draws to mind the example of St. Francis.[23] He says that "the harmony which Saint Francis of Assisi experienced with all creatures was seen as a healing of that rupture [of sin]" and that "through universal reconciliation with every creature, Saint Francis in some way returned to the state of original innocence."[24] Through the healing of sin, we can also heal the wounds in creation. This is a call to radical personal holiness. Just as St. Francis left the riches of his life to live a life of holy poverty, so we too are called to live a life of holy poverty and not follow the ways of the world. We cannot just pass off the responsibility to care for creation to someone else since we do not pollute as much as them. We must recognize that our sin is what is destroying creation, and so repentance, reconciliation, and a life of holiness are the responsibility of each and every one of us.

However, because the problem also regards the secondary causes by which our sin destroys the world, these must be dealt with as well. Since the climate is a common good, Pope Francis calls upon the institution which has care of the common good, the political community.[25] As Suarez points out, this has to be established because man is by nature created as a social animal as we see in Genesis. The ecological crisis requires policies at the international, national, and local levels, in accordance with the principles of both solidarity and subsidiarity.

If we wish then to take the message of *Laudato Si'* seriously, we must call the liberal state to repentance for its sins: for denying the laborer his wage, for destroying the environment, for slaughtering the unborn, for destroying the family, and most of all for refusing to

---

[21] C.f. *LS* 2.

[22] This is not to say Adam's sin actually changes the natures of things, but rather that he disorders their interrelation. What exactly the effects of Adam's sin are on the creation is an important area for future research in theology.

[23] *LS* 10-12.

[24] *LS* 66.

[25] *LS* 163-198.

acknowledge the Creator and the true faith he established. Pope Francis wrote this encyclical to "all people" because all people, not just the faithful of the Church, are bound to listen to the Church when it speaks.[26] The modern world must abandon its idolatry and submit to Christ and his Roman Pontiff.

It is extremely important to combat these new creation myths that have come about and to return to the teachings of scripture and the tradition as the Church has always expounded them. If we just come to scripture with our own opinions on what it means, we could take Genesis to mean anything and perhaps even use it to justify modern creation myths and use it to justify committing sins. However, we have to understand it as is taught by the tradition and the magisterium. We see the tradition and the magisterium returns again and again to Genesis to illustrate the importance of creation for modern social issues and most especially for the ecological crisis that we face today.

---

[26] *LS* 3.

5

The Importance of the Theology of Creation in the Field of Bioethics

Vito Čapeta

Bioethics is an interdisciplinary field that examines the moral and ethical issues related to the life sciences, medicine, biomedical research, and technologies that involve human beings and the environment in light of rational moral principles.[1] It seeks to address complex ethical dilemmas that arise due to scientific and technological advancements in the biological and medical sciences. It became clear that addressing these complex issues could not be left solely to doctors but required the involvement of various experts, including philosophers, theologians, and legal scholars, in the analysis and discussion of topics such as abortion, in vitro fertilization, euthanasia, end-of-life care, organ transplantation, and clinical experimentation. The theology of creation should be the source and pinnacle in every aspect of bioethics to promote a comprehensive and compassionate humanism.

I. Law and Bioethics

Law and the world of legislation are connected to the theology of creation in bioethics. Human rights represent a set of goods that, in every historical moment, embody the requirements of dignity, freedom, and equality, which must be positively recognized by national and international legal systems. These fundamental human rights include the right to life, the right to freedom, the right to health, and the right to physical integrity. All these goods are embraced by the right to dignity, from which they derive. The right of all rights is the right to life, the fundamental principle on which not only social life is built but also the legal order itself. All of this has a common denominator known as natural law.

Natural law is what is just before any process of legal

---

[1] G. M. Comolli, *Manuale di bioetica l'uomo deal XX secolo*, 25, http://www.gianmariacomolli.it/wp-content/uploads/2019/08/CLICCA-QUI-E-SCARICA-IL-MANUALE-COMPLETO-IN-PDF.pdf.

formulation—for example, the right to life and freedom are not just because legitimate authority has promulgated them but because they are naturally right for every human being from the moment of their existence. Legitimate authority does not grant these rights; it recognizes them from the natural law. Laws are just to the extent that they reflect these fundamental rights derived from the dignity of the human being, which finds its foundation in the divine image and likeness.

Natural law should illuminate positive laws. According to St. Thomas, the law is "the ordering of reason promulgated by legitimate authority for the common good."[2] We can distinguish between moral law and civil law. Civil law is structured in a pyramid form where, at the top, we have a constitution, then international treaties/laws, and then national laws (e.g. civil, criminal, health). This is the horizontal dimension of law. It is not enough to have the horizontal dimension of laws to regulate human behavior in light of rational principles; These laws structured in this way (Constitution – International Laws – National Laws) are not an end in themselves; civil laws find their perfection in the revelation of divine law and in the Ten Commandments, which find their perfection in the Word of God the Father Creator – Jesus Christ, who gave us the Law of Love – Love God with all your heart, soul, and strength and love your neighbor as yourself.

The ultimate purpose of the law is the administration of justice for the common good, linked to the transcendent values of truth, justice, freedom, and the promotion of fundamental human rights, which include the right to life, freedom, and health. In the measure that each law respects the fundamental dimension of human existence we conform to that law.

Moral law presupposes the existence of God, the Creator who created human nature: "Do good, avoid evil."[3] This is the law written in the heart of every person. So, who can be the true author, the true moral legislator? Only Him. Because, having created human beings, each of us, He gives us and makes known to us those laws that, by obeying them, we reach our true good both as individuals and as a society. Today, on the contrary, we live in an era that is against the Creator God because humanity, more than being a steward, has

---

[2] Thomas Aquinas, *Summa theologiae*, I-II, q. 90, a. 4.
[3] C.f. *ST*, I-II, q. 94, a. 2.

become a master of creation. It wants to manage its own existence. Consequently, laws are created that are not in line with the law of the Creator God because they do not promote the fundamental goods derived from human dignity, such as the right to life, health (i.e. physical, psychological, spiritual), and freedom. Therefore, we have laws that allow assisted suicide, abortion, surrogacy, and the modification of one's body according to one's pleasure. Man chooses when to be born and how and when to die.

There is an anthropology that is not personalistic but reductionist. Without bioethics based on the theology of creation, the vision of man is based solely on his intellectual and volitional capacities and his efficiency, and therefore the man that cannot contribute to society is being suggested rather not to live and to choose euthanasia as the way out. can be no healthy medicine and laws that regulate human behavior towards true freedom, justice, and benevolence. Our society has eclipsed the "sense of God," and consequently, the value of man has faded. In the words of the Second Vatican Council, "without the Creator the creature would disappear… When God is forgotten, however, the creature itself grows unintelligible."[4] Saint John Paul II, commenting upon this passage, says that, "once all reference to God has been removed, it is not surprising that the meaning of everything else becomes profoundly distorted. Nature itself, from being 'mater' (mother), is now reduced to being 'matter', and is subjected to every kind of manipulation."[5]

Therefore, a bioethicist must be able to navigate the legislative landscape in order to protect life. For this purpose, legislative knowledge helps them, naturally finding its foundation and perfection not only in the constitution but in divine law, which inspires the constitution and laws of lower rank. In this form, laws aim at peace, social cohesion, the common good, and humanity. The theology of creation illuminates ethical-legal criteria and, consequently, actions in the field of life and health. Legal issues are often intertwined with ethical issues in the biomedical field, and then bioethical issues raise questions of a spiritual and religious nature. Deontological codes and the behavior of physicians toward patients go in different directions, whether it is end-of-life cases, medically assisted procreation, or CRISPR, sterilization.

---

[4] *Gaudium et spes* 36; c.f. John Paul II, *Evangelium vitae* 22; CCC 49; Comolli 71.
[5] *Evangelium vitae* 22; c.f. Comolli 71.

II. The Role of Theology in Bioethics

For the Catholic perspective, there exists the paradigm of the sacredness of life, articulated in three fundamental principles: creation by God, the non-negotiability and inviolability of human life. Nevertheless, life is not considered an absolute value, as the most important thing for believers would be what awaits them after death. However, in the natural law tradition of Thomism, life, being a gift, could not be the subject of utilitarian speculations. The contribution of theology to bioethics lies in the concept of the dignity and equality of all human beings, a concept that was not known before. It was present from the very beginning: God created every human being starting from Adam and Eve with a plan by which He created every human being in His image and likeness. Therefore, we are all created by the same God, and thus, we are all equal. Then Christianity introduced the novel concept of disinterested charity, even to the extent of loving one's enemy. Not just friends, not just those who do good to you. This was a novelty, a revolution. Justice consists of giving each person their due and returning what belongs to them. Giving what belongs to the other. Charity, on the other hand, is giving the other what is mine! It's not that I owe the other an equal amount. We must be like the Good Samaritan.

The concept of the person arises within theological reflection, from the fourth and fifth centuries, culminating in the definition by Boethius in the sixth century. The term "person," which originally meant a mask, came to signify a human being as well as divine persons: "an individual substance of a rational nature."[6] This concept was developed by theology from the Latin term *persona* and the Greek *prosopon*.

Thus, a human being is not a "thing" but a "who." The perspective starts from the unified creation of the human being, who is both body and spirit because both dimensions are created by the same God. It is God who also creates the body. The body is not pure matter: the person is a spiritualized body and an incarnated soul. Everything is created, everything is a design of God, and everything is respected in fullness.

There exists what we can call a metaphysical passivity with which the body is marked. Having a body means being called into existence, being

---

[6] Boethius, *Liber de persona et duabus naturis contra Eutychen et Nestorium*, line 35, https://www.perseus.tufts.edu/hopper/text?doc=Perseus%3Atext%3A2008.01.0677%3Aloebline%3Dpos%3D41.

in the world with specific weight and height that we did not choose. This passivity also speaks of the awareness that life is received as a gift, without merit on the part of the recipient. It is an accepted mystery that helps us live and become ourselves without denying or rejecting the giver.[7]

The human body is very significant in bioethics:

For these reasons, it can be said that the body cannot be observed separately but speaks of the human being as a whole entity, as a relational being. The body is not something separate from me, but I am that body expressing itself in various ways depending on its condition. It is not an object or a system but the presence of being, the unified center of life, and the original givenness that is conveyed through a smile, a kiss, a touch, a facial expression, and so on. All of this indicates the other as an indivisible and free other.[8]

This should inspire decisions in bioethics.

Every life is sacred, even specifically in the view of medicine, the medical profession, the Hippocratic physician, and the followers of Galen. From the perspective of the theology of creation, medicine is not just Hippocratic but even more so, the physician is a follower of Christ the physician, who healed souls as well as bodies. Thus, medicine is viewed as a diaconate, not just a virtue-based attitude in service of the patient but a diaconate, a service that extends even to the sickest, or the leper who was cast aside—Jesus received them, healed them, touched them. This created a revolution, leading to the establishment of hospitals to receive the sick, pilgrims, etc. Today, we can speak of palliative care.

III. Bioethics and the Issue of Death

Death is a broad and profound phenomenon that is approached from medical, legal, philosophical, social, and religious perspectives.

Death from the medical point of view is identified with the "irreversible cessation of all functions of the encephalon."[9] Basically, the death of the encephalic tissue coincides with the death of the individual. The irreversible cessation of the encephalon leads to the

---

[7] D. Rad, *Teološko-bioetičko vrjednovanje transhumanističke antropologije*, 193.
[8] Rad, 193.
[9] L. D'Antonio, *Aspetti Medico legati all'accertaento di morte*, accessed February 27, 2024,
https://www.trapianti.salute.gov.it/imgs/C_17_cntPubblicazioni_514_allegato.pdf.

cessation of the functioning of the organism because encephalon is the main organ that is responsible for the integration of the whole organism.[10] So the ability to interact with environment, sensations, perception, language, consciousness, knowledge have their dependence and departure in the encephalon. If encephalon does not function, then irreversible termination of the whole organism happens and thus death of the person. How can we understand that the structures of the encephalon are dead? How is the diagnosis understood? Absence of electrical signals, tissue does not function, if tissue functions, then it causes the presence of electrical signals.

In fact, electroencephalogram only describes activity of the cortex, but does not describe the activity of other parts of the central nervous system. There is also subcortical area (under cortex) that is investigated through cranial nerve activity.

Cranial nerves originate in the brainstem, and if there are no reflexes from these cranial peers, then it means the brainstem is dead = total absence of brain reflexes. Cranial nerves are important from a bioethical point of view to constate encephalic death: for example, if in front of light the pupils do not react. And I can get if 1, 2, 3, is not there I can say everything is ruined and diagnose encephalic death. The Law of the Rules of the Determination and Certification of Death of December 29, 1993 No. 578 ART 1 defines encephalic death as the "irreversible cessation of all functions of the encephalon."[11]

Another indicator of death is absence of spontaneous breathing. (Apnea tests are done in which ventilation is taken off and to see if the respiratory centers respond and if this does not happen it means the core of the brain center is dead). What are the causes of death from a physiological point of view? We eventually die because one of these three things is missing: Loss of respiratory function, loss of heartbeat, neurological cause-primarily neurological alterations involving the respiratory centers.

From a philosophical point of view, we can say that the human person is unique being who not only dies, but knows that he or she dies. Now the person is created and composed in three dimensions which are that of body, psyche and spirit. Now death means the end of

---

[10] Á. R. Luño, "Rapporti tra il concetto filosofico e il concetto clinico di morte," *Acta Philosophica* 1, no. 1 (1992): 54-68.
[11] L. D'Antonio.

this temporal life. The phenomenon of death accompanies all people, from the perspective of Aristotelian-Thomistic philosophy, death consists of the separation of body and soul. During life the personal body and soul form substantial unity of the human being. St. Thomas says that the human soul is subsistent because it has being in itself. The body receives being of the soul.[12] Every living being preserves unity through its own operations: its unity is so fundamental that, if it is lost, death, that is, the end of life, occurs.[13] When man dies, a substantial change takes place; the separation of body and soul. In fact, the separation of body and soul after death is not the end of personal life. Death marks the end of the temporality of the body, but not the end of personal life. The personal human soul has the spiritual principle in it, and precisely because of this spiritual dimension, the human soul subsists after death, and personal life continues. The soul is not only incorruptible because of its complete immateriality, but it cannot cease to be since it possesses a spiritual being. What does it mean that soul is spiritual? That it has intelligence, will and memory, the capacity for abstraction, negation, reflexivity in which immateriality is given, characterized by transcendence over the environment and the organic body. All these things subsist after death.

We are not born to die, but we die to live. Jesus conquered death and rose again in body and soul, and this is the source of hope for every Christian. "Christ won this victory when He rose to life, for by His death He freed man from death."[14] So, death for us Christians is the "passage" from earthly life to heavenly life. As Our Lord says, "In my Father's house are many rooms; if it were not so, would I have told you that I go to prepare a place for you? And when I go and prepare a place for you, I will come again and will take you to myself, that where I am you may be also. And you know the way where I am going" (John 14:2-4). Death is not a tragedy, because the greatest tragedy is the loss of fellowship with God. Therefore, we are not afraid, for we know that "our commonwealth is in heaven, and from it we await a Savior, the Lord Jesus Christ, who will change our lowly body to be like his glorious body, by the power which enables him even to subject all things to himself" (Phil 3:20-21).

---

[12] Thomas Aquinas, *In De Anima*, a. 14, ad. 10.
[13] A. Lombo and F. Russo, *Antropologia filosofica una introduzione*, (Edusc, 2007).
[14] *Gaudium et spes* 18.

IV. Bioethics, Technology, and Cloning

Science should not lose sight of theology. Nowadays, modern technologies are an inevitable part of our current and future way of life. However, within the context of theological-moral reflection, it makes no sense to ban everything that stems from these technologies. Instead, it is important to warn, caution, and promote responsible innovation starting from the mystery of man, which can only be understood in the person of Jesus Christ. He confers on every individual complete dignity and a bright future. This mysterious truth does not tolerate that man is an object but rather a subject to be respected and defended in every circumstance and place (e.g., laws, constitution, rights as mentioned above). The pursuit of a better life can never be justified by technological achievements that deny that dignity founded on the creation of man in the image of God. This does not mean that theology is a moral engineer imposing its veto on technological advancements that continue on their path. The role of theology is to awaken consciousness and morality regarding the paths taken by these advancements, which in many cases demonstrate progress in subtly and cunningly destroying humanity and the created world.

A clear example of the need for theology in bioethics can be found in cloning. Cloning is the asexual and agamic reproduction in the laboratory of the genetic makeup of a living being characterized by the same genetic information as the first, that is, a pair that is genetically identical to its progenitor.[15] Put simply, cloning is medical intervention that consists of producing an individual identical to another individual, and this act is carried out in the laboratory.

At the technical level, cloning can be done in two ways: The first technique of cloning is called embryiospliting. The word "splitting" means an operation whereby from a single embryo of 4 or 8 cells, by isolating individual cells, 4 or 8 embryos can be obtained. Technically this mode can be called cloning by embryo splitting. The second technique is called cloning proper. In this type of production of the genetically identical individuals the key role plays the action of nuclear transfer. This involves two steps: first egg cell or unicellular embryo is enucleated, then the cell whose nucleus is to be transferred is fused with the new egg or unicellular embryo by electric shock

---

[15] Comolli.

which, precisely, allows meeting of these two biological materials and thus new embryo is created.[16] All types of cloning have as a common effect the prediction of embryos and the destruction of embryos or freezing of embryos.

Human cloning is absolutely prohibited by European, national and international regulations. However, there are some people who are in favor of cloning. Some people defend cloning because it allows the possibility of transplantable organs from frozen embryos, replicating gifted individuals from sports, scientific, aesthetic fields, giving children to infertile couples or those with hereditary diseases, and improving IVF techniques. However, the majority of contemporary society is not in favor of cloning, as many see it as an attack on individuality and integrity, a disrespect for dignity, a violation of personal freedom, and because the human being would come to be considered and appreciated only according to his origin and not in himself.

It is ethics that should guide science and not vice versa. The Pontifical Academy for Life that cloning "represents a radical manipulation of the constitutive relationality and complementarity which is at the origin of human procreation in both its biological and strictly personal aspects."[17] Saint John Paul II likewise states that, "begetting is the continuation of Creation."[18] The child, the new human being is a gift, not a product.

Human cloning perverts the fundamental relationships of the human person: filiation, consanguinity, parenting, number of children sacrificed. Such deconstruction involves the redefinition of human identity tout court.

God the Creator's call to be fruitful and multiply must be done responsibly and in accordance with his laws. "God saw everything that he had made, and behold, it was very good" (Gen 1:31). Every child (and also every creature) is born from an origin that gives without bounds, from a love that is unconditional. We must respect the gift of creation. At stake is not only an ethical attitude, but also ontological love. Humanae Vitae affirms "inseparable connection" between unitive and procreative meaning of the conjugal act and consequently

---

[16] Appuni delle lezioni – Interventi medici AA. 2023/24.
[17] Pontifical Academia for Life, *Reflections on Cloning*, 3.
[18] *Evangelium vitae* 43.

the "unlawfulness" of all artificial methods of birth control.[19] Cloning denies the unitive meaning between man and woman. Let us not forget that every man is created by God in His image and likeness, as a unique and unrepeatable individual and not programmed in the laboratory (c.f. Gen 1:17). Therefore, the Catholic Church deplores cloning, as it is a science devoid of values. Cloning by reducing man to the level of a product is totally incompatible with his dignity and risks being a tragic parody of God's omnipotence.[20] This act represents a great insult to God the Creator by human pride.[21]

It is clear that man cannot evaluate himself based on technology but on what truly makes him human. Man has no source or meaning in himself or in his products but in God, Jesus Christ. Technology is called to necessarily open up to a theological perspective that highlights the socially recognized loss of the sense of transcendence through a gradual and certainly progressive confrontation with the biblical conception of the world, nature, and man as works of creation and salvation by God. Theological thought should expose the dictatorship of "scientific-natural rationality, technical efficiency, economic greed, and calculation, all flavored with (hyper)social sensitivity to material well-being."[22]

Even though contemporary converging technology offers a certain "soteriology," it cannot provide man with the fundamental meaning of life and the happiness he ardently desires. Biblical faith offers man answers not only to achieve this happiness but also guidelines for bioethics because theology and faith offer: the correct action (technique) and inspiration for a right life (ethics). Created in the image of God, man finds answers to existential questions not only in technology guided by the logic of efficiency and utility but also in the humble discovery of the mystery of a world created by the love and care of God. Man is not a mere object for scientific, clinical, and technical experiments but is open to transcendence, which means that he is called to establish a relationship with God and to be a faithful steward of the goods, considering that he is the greatest good among creatures and not a being to be subjugated to the world and creatures.

---

[19] Paul VI, *Humanae vitae* 12-14.
[20] Pontifical Academy for Life, *Reflections on Cloning*.
[21] C.f. Comolli.
[22] Rad, 193.

V. Conclusion

All of this shows us that Catholic bioethics is based on the theology of creation and on faith and reason.: The relationship of faith to reason is like an eye to a telescope. If I go out in the evening and perhaps see the stars, very few of them, if I then take a telescope, I discover a world I did not see before. Many more stars, much brighter, but I have to put the telescope in front of my eye, and if I put it in front of my ear, I see nothing. That is, I have to use my capacity to see, but I enhance it with the instrument. Similarly, the theology of creation is enhanced by bioethics and its interdisciplinarity. It amplifies, so I have to reason concretely in ethics. One source of moral analysis is reason, but not only reason but also scripture, the tradition of the Magisterium, and reason as such. But I can enhance my ability to reason—with the telescope in front of my eye, faith in front of reason to reason better and see more deeply. But even the theology of creation needs bioethics to expand and discover all its richness and applicability and its necessity in the world in which we live to direct ourselves towards the Creator God from whom and for whom we are created.

6

Regenerative Agriculture and the Practical Implications of Genesis 1

Shawn and Beth Dougherty

Then God said, "Let us make mankind in our image, in our likeness, so that they may rule over the fish in the sea and the birds in the sky, over the livestock and all the wild animals, and over all the creatures that move along the ground."

So God created mankind in his own image, in the image of God he created them; male and female he created them.

God blessed them and said to them, "Be fruitful and increase in number, fill the earth and subdue it. Rule over the fish in the sea and the birds in the sky and over every living creature that moves on the ground."

God saw all that he had made, and it was very good. (Genesis 1: 26-28, 31)

****

Let us note that at the glorious and unsullied moment of creation, Man is given the vocation to care for the natural world. Even in its unequivocally blessed state, creation is in need of care, and the enactment of that care is an unequivocal blessing for our sinless first parents. They like work.

They have been created with insight, foresight, strength, and dexterity, and placed in a bountiful, ebullient Nature. Its gifts and propensities are accessible to their understanding. They can see what it is made for, and envision ways to draw from it an even greater beauty, an even more sublime order, and even richer abundance; and when they move to enact these visions, Nature responds willingly to their suggestion.

Nature likes them.

One might ask why, in an unfallen creation, Nature should have any need of oversight; why, before our first disobedience, all was not in a completed state of perfection? Well, we are not theologians, but it seems obvious to us that our first parents were created for and called to a collaborative subordinate creativity, with God, and that the rest of creation, over which we have dominion, and which we are to 'till' and 'subdue', are the joyful objects of our co-creativity. The completion of the nature of Nature will be realized in the forms it achieves in response to our creativity.

In simple language, we would say that Adam and Eve wanted to work, and viewed that work as a joy, the way Mozart wanted to make music and took joy in composing.

In any case, a joyful but unguided prelapserian natural world certainly would be in need of direction, despite the lack of disease, drought, or predation. Animals and plants lack insight and forethought. Plant placement, grazing patterns, breeding choices, reproductive rates, are all susceptible to improvement or enhancement by the application of Man's creativity and wisdom.

And while animals are the natural effectors of landscape alteration – by grazing, browsing, rooting, digging, earth-moving, dam building and so on – they cannot will or direct the comprehensive results of their work, individually or collectively. Being conformable to the will of our first parents, however, they became collaborators in Man's vision for the Garden. With the help of animals, Man's training and cultivation of the natural world would have reached levels now unimaginable.

Among the co-creative undertakings of an unfallen world, there would also have been the pleasures of enhancing the provision and placement of growing things, either for beauty, as in the work of Gertrude Jekyll or Capability Brown, or for the delight of provision, as it might be, growing walnuts beside figs for the pleasure of harvesting and eating them together.

Hybridization, and the possibilities of enhancement by pruning, would have been creative delights available in an unfallen world.

Listen again to God's language: 'Let us make mankind, in our likeness, so that they may rule, fill the earth and subdue it.' It is, then, our primary vocation, that for which we were called and created, that which makes us like God, to rule and to tame the things of the earth.

How are we doing? Have we gotten lost somewhere along the way?

****

With our Fall from grace, Nature changed catastrophically. The created world is no longer harmonious; Adam and Eve lack much of their original insight, and much of their innate authority. Simultaneously, Man's call to cocreativity becomes on a practical level much more urgent. In a profound shift, Adam is faced now with seasonality; no longer do the plants bear fruit in every season. The ground is cursed; now, when Adam so clearly needs to have dominion, he has lost much of his gift for the task. The animals have lost their conformity to his desires. His labor will produce thistles and thorns.

Dwelling in a created world that no longer responds harmoniously to his will, Adam has to make provision to feed himself and his wife. His offspring will have to do the same. No longer a collaboration with Nature for which both Nature and man are divinely gifted, this provision will now consist, at least in part, of force and resistance. We still need to receive from nature the means to meet our physical requirements, but our mastery and judgement are now impaired; our choices will be less appropriate, and our means to carry them out, less efficacious. Furthermore, in a situation requiring new depths of patience, we have already demonstrated an unwillingness to practice personal restraint.

We are no longer entirely at home in the natural world; there will be a tension between what Nature will do for us naturally, and what we will require from Nature in violation of nature.

****

Since Man's eviction from the Garden, farming has fallen more or less into one of two patterns. In most cases, and for the longest periods, farming has taken the form of some kind of ecosystem management. That is to say, any agricultural methods or activities in a given place drew their form and function from the place itself – from the soil, topography, climate, and the native plants and animals. For example, where soils were deep and fertile and rains gentle and well-spaced, grain and pulses played a major role in the food culture. Where soils were shallow and rocky, vines were common. In hot climates olives, figs, and dates featured largely in the human diet. Grass, the common denominator, was everywhere harvested by domestic herbivores for meat and milk.

The reason is simple: Man, setting out to grow food or feedstocks, would naturally elect to grow crops closely related to the plants the land was already producing. He needs to make a crop, and nothing would be more likely to thrive than the plant families that had already self-selected for the place. Naturally so; he depends for survival on making a harvest, and where it is possible to hedge a bet, we hedge a bet; particularly if the stakes are life and death.

It follows that Man's regional agricultural methods would be designed to reproduce the conditions nature already provides for the wild plant relatives of his domestic food crops that are flourishing in a place: fertile, loamy soils for grains; steady moisture for nightshade relatives like tomatoes, peppers, eggplants; acid soil for cucumbers and garlic.

This kind of farming is *Biomimicry.*

Biomimicry is susceptible of great creativity and enhancement. Alternating crops so leguminous, nitrogen-fixing species store fertility for heavy-feeding crops like corn, is an example of biomimicry. The rotation of livestock in daily moves over pasture imitates the migration of wild herbivores. Discovering that rice tolerates saturated soils – a rare plant trait – we flood paddies to grow rice weed-free. By providing Asian jungle fowl with constant access to easy calories, we are able to multiply their reproductive window by a large factor.

Biomimicry is our attempt to nurture what is left, after the Fall, of our original, divine gift for tending the earth.

The second of the two patterns of farming can be defined in contrast to the first; we may call it *Force.* Where Biomimicry works with and within natural limitations, Force proposes to eliminate them. It can attempt to do this with a simple disregard for more remote negative results, as imperial Rome's shiploads of slave-grown Carthaginian grain fed hungry citizens at home, while they were a driving force behind the desertification of north Africa. Or, as ever-more powerful technology replaces – or redefines – human slavery, Force can attempt to enact an alternative world in which there *are* no unavoidable negative results, no natural limitations. In this case, human invention is employed without restraint; adverse response is to be nullified instantly by ever greater manipulation, each subsequent level further advancing whatever human goal is being pursued. No consideration is given to subsidiary or corollary costs, for as long as it is possible to ignore them.

In commercial agriculture – therefore, in almost any agricultural undertaking in the industrialized world – Force is the mode of virtually all of our still-necessary interactions with the living, natural world. We are using force to wrest a tremendous harvest from the supine earth. But there is a cost to this violence; with every season, the price tag is going up. Soil loss; toxicity of air, water and soil; loss of the genetic diversity that once provided resilience in our food crops; earthshaking food-related reductions in human health; these are all part of that price tag.

History shows us that for many centuries, humans looked for ways to manage land so that it would feed them and go on feeding them. When they succeeded – and our presence on the planet in great numbers and on every continent argues that it frequently, overwhelmingly succeeded – it was because they managed the land, plants and animals according to natural patterns. When humans have ignored those patterns, they have died. There is a lesson to be learned here: Observe the limitations of Nature and, within those limitations, Nature will feed you; violate those limitations and the same principles that gave you plenty, will give you famine.

It is a lesson that the coercive power of the lever, the internal combustion engine, and a glut of petroleum have allowed mankind temporarily to forget. The industrial revolution has, for the past century, provided us with the means to force from Nature an almost unthinkable, if temporary, increase in productivity. As we have developed more and more complex and powerful technologies, Force has made it possible to select agricultural goals that violate not only natural limits, but Nature itself. From the Dust Bowl to genetic engineering is a gap of less than fifty years.

Nevertheless, with all our irresistible persuasion, we have not succeeded in developing a system to *replace* Nature; only to coerce it. We have still to reckon with the nature of Nature. Plants must capture sunlight and convert it to complex hydrocarbons for the use of other living things. All food production depends upon some transaction of this kind. Long-term, there is no alternative means of procuring energy for life.

✳✳✳✳✳✳✳✳✳✳✳✳✳✳✳✳✳✳✳✳✳

Never in history has any people been so divided – in physical distance, in knowledge, in skill – from its own means of survival. The American dinner, we are told, travels an average of 1500 miles from farm to table. Fewer than 1% of Americans identify themselves as farmers. The average age of these is almost 60, which, we are told, is also their average life expectancy – a grim correspondence. Our time seems to be running out.

Were we enjoying a stable and peaceful civilization, such divisions would still be perilous. Our civilization is not stable, it is not peaceful, and under such circumstances the fragility and attenuation of our means of food provision are breathtaking.

We are living now in a place and at a time in which the majority of people have no cultural memory of farming and no personal experience of the natural patterns that make farming possible. Food provision takes the form of a foray to the grocery store or the placement of an online order to be delivered to our door. Factory farming seems, to most people, to be working; their hunting and gathering expeditions are always and easily successful.

The average person does not see and is not personally aware of the cropland erosion that costs us, according to Wendell Berry, two bushels of Iowa topsoil for each bushel of corn.

The average person does not see and is seldom aware that the genetically modified corn he consumes, directly, in 80% of processed foods, and in the forms of almost any commercial meat or dairy product, is itself a registered pesticide.

He is not aware that three-quarters of the processed foods he consumes contain measurable amounts of the carcinogenic herbicide glyphosate.

He seldom has more than a few days' calories in his home at any time.

He has never kept a garden, raised a laying hen, or cut up a chicken carcass.

When it comes to food, without the commercial food industry the average American is completely dependent upon an attenuated, complicated, cumbersome agglomeration of heavy equipment, compacted, sterile soil, cloned, genetically modified monocrops, pollution, contamination, processing, packaging, shipping, and retailing, all designed not to feed us well and securely but to siphon off the largest possible portion of our food dollars to fill the pockets of the smallest possible number of corporations while allowing us the least possible information about how any of this comes about. WE are abjectly helpless in the matter of our own food; we know little about how it comes to be, and nothing about how to affect a change in the process.

And let us say again: factory farming does not work. It is at best a temporary violence wresting a temporary surfeit of calories from dead soil artificially invigorated with fossil energy. It is powered by mechanical and chemical energy in enormous disproportion to the food energy produced. Simple accounting, of caloric deficit or of ecological deficit, is enough to demonstrate the hemorrhagic nature of our food production system.

****

Dire as this situation is, it is symptomatic of an even greater calamity: Man's almost complete alienation from his original God-given vocation and mandate of responsibility for the physical, earthly creation.

It is reasonable to ask whether we are by our present industrial food system enacting any part of our original calling. Whether we consider food, shelter, clothing, or any other of the items we now consider needs, we live by issuing a proxy to the industrial economy to despoil the earth on our behalf. The average twentieth-century citizen of the industrialized world has no knowledge of, and takes no thought for, the task for which we are naturally, divinely created: God's mandate to have dominion over the earth. 'Nature', the living physical creation, is for most people almost exclusively a visual stimulus, often experienced only virtually; it is in no way a personal responsibility.

This has been the case for several generations, and few people give it any thought. But if we offer ourselves any excuse for the omission – and we seldom feel the need to do so – It has become a commonplace to tell ourselves that farming by proxy has been strictly necessary, that all ages prior to the industrial revolution lived ever on the verge of starvation, that small-scale farming, subsistence farming, is miserable and precarious, and therefore untenable by any intelligent race or civilization; in other words, that industrialized, mechanized, chemicalized farming, farming done by a tiny few on behalf of the consuming masses, is the only safe, only reliable, only reasonable means by which we may make provision; that, in short, industrialized farming is necessary. And, if necessary, necessarily good, or at worst a necessary evil.

The logical conclusion must in that case be that in fact we *have* no divine vocation to earth care; or that this vocation, in a post-Fall world, is a vocation to slavery, most desirable to be avoided. All things are for the best in this best of all possible worlds. And in any case, is there any other option?

There is.

****

Any serious discussion of a divine ecology of food – of a God-given order meant to provide a pattern for Man's working relationship with the natural, living world from which he takes his life – can only be undertaken if we first come to an understanding of the conditions that define that relationship. To know how we ought to be providing our food, we must first ask, how does food come to be?

This part of our discussion might be considered *an explanation of the necessity of the pastoral.*

All life energy is some permutation of the energy of the sun, collected, converted, and stored in green leaves. The sun shines; plants grow; every other living thing depends on this transaction. Soil is built up out of the bodies of dead plants and animals, and living plants hold the soil in place and photosynthesize.

The immeasurably complex interconnection of all the living things in any given environment– what Wendell Berry prefers to term a *neighborhood* – is the structure through which the captured solar energy travels in an effectively endless loop, beginning with, and returning through, green plant life. Encountering this complexity, Man has a choice.

Industrial man employs Force – chemical, mechanical, and now genetic – to mine this energy for his own use.

But there is an alternative. Coming to any place with an extant community of volunteer plant life – an ecosystem, if you will – we can first *admire*, we can 'look with wonder'. In this looking, we note an intact, effective, durable, solar-energy-and-rainwater-capture pathway made up of living things. This ecosystem is in some way sustainable, regenerative; that's why it's here.

Admiring it, we can value its health, its 'whole-ness'. Valuing this, we will ask, not, how can we mine the energy so laid down, but, how can we conserve and become a contributing part of this pathway?

The answer is right under our feet.

It is *grass,* or more specifically that myriad assortment of herbaceous, mostly perennial ground-covers, both grasses and forbs, that make up Earth's grasslands. Call it pasture or forage, covering 40% of the Earth's landmass, grasslands are the largest ecosystem type on the planet. And over and above sheer quantity, grass has qualities that make it the most essential element in our food pathways.

This importance is primal. First, because grass is so ubiquitous, available in enormous quantities almost anywhere humans have been able to live.

Secondly, by the physiological nature of this community of herbaceous ground covers. Pasture plants comprise hundreds of species which collect sunlight with leaves of unimaginable variety in shape, size, color, height, texture, and orientation. Together they are so efficient a trap for photons that in healthy grasslands, little measurable light reaches the soil surface. Grass is *efficient*.

Thirdly, because it is natural and appropriate to such plants to be grazed. Simply put, they *benefit* from natural grazing; in many or most cases, they even require it. Good grazing triggers plant regrowth while building soil; it improves the plant community and soil fertility by the same means that feeds the grazing herds. Grass and grazing are, at least in potential, an unqualified good.

In any natural plant community that is not entirely wooded, then, the primal, renewable energy source is grass. The only difficulty is that it's mostly cellulose, and we can't digest it.

Fortunately, we partner with animal species that can. Cows, sheep, and goats are among the animal genera that *can* digest cellulose, turning it into forms that are abundantly useful to human beings, among them meat, milk, and fiber – not to mention manure, which restores with interest the fertility of the soil from which the grass grew. So grass, under the right conditions, feeds not only animals and humans, but, in feeding the soil, is the best possible guarantee that the animals and humans will go on being fed. In other words, given proper care, there *is* such a thing as a free lunch.

All post-Fall human inhabitance of this planet – and much of the animal inhabitance as well – has had at its foundation this symbiotic relationship between herbaceous ground covers and the herbivores that eat them. Hunter-gatherer communities follow behind migratory herds in a remote management grazing program; pastoral tribes managed domestic herds more directly.

Before the Industrial Revolution, land renewal methods were developed over centuries that restored land fertility by rotating through periods of 'field, fold, and fallow'. Alternating land use between cropping, meadow, and pasture acknowledges that while land degrades under the plow, grasslands, especially grazed grasslands, build fertility naturally. Sunlight, harvested by plant leaves, supplies the necessary organic matter; soil life, fed by the organic matter, provides nitrogen and micronutrients to grow more plants.

In the 20th century the Haber-Bosch process enabled man to synthesize ammonia by the combustion of natural gas under high pressure. This has resulted in the rapid and by now almost complete substitution of artificial and chemical fertilizers for natural soil amendments, but that this is not a long-term alternative is patently obvious.

First, because chemical fertilizers damage soil life and cannot replace its services.

Secondly, because its use has resulted in continuous cropping, eliminating the fallow periods during which in previous times soil structure was restored and erosion controlled.

Thirdly, because it substitutes a finite, non-renewable resource produced at great expense of energy for one that is effectively infinite, constant and self-perpetuating.

A fourth reason which has become evident in recent decades is the radical decline in nutritional value of foods produced using these reductive industrial methods. Evidence for this diminishment is everywhere; among the most dramatic are the recent crises in human health most noteworthy in those places where agriculture has become most industrialized. We have no historic precedent for the widespread incidences of obesity, heart disease, diabetes, hypertension, cancers of all sorts, asthma, allergies, and autoimmune diseases, as well as mental and developmental illnesses of epidemic proportions. Statistical human longevity maintained by the application of a previously unthinkable dedication of human labor in the form of drugs, surgeries and therapies, is not to be used as evidence of human prosperity.

We have to conclude that an agriculture that draws its energy, both for tillage and for productivity, from fossil sunlight in the form of petroleum-derived fuel, fertilizer, pesticides, and herbicides, has not been successful. Petrochemically-derived fertility has at least two fatal problems: it is limited, and it is toxic. It is evident that only contemporary sunlight can be relied upon to supply contemporary fertility. Artificial fertilizers cannot replace manures.

Additionally, while frequent tillage is destructive of soil structure and fertility, perennial grasslands under well-managed grazing are beneficial to both. Put another way: cropping is hard on land; good grazing regenerates land.

So much for the use of Force and our tractor-petroleum-and-row-crop-based industrial ag system. What remains is Biomimicry, and the return to ecologically managed grasslands and grazing animals.

Which means a return to farming with the local genius, and farming on the human scale.

****

Our family has spent the past quarter-century farming and living on seventeen acres of wasteland in northern Appalachia, land officially designated by the state of Ohio 'not suitable for agriculture'. For the past twelve years we have also been managing thirty acres of stripped hilltop belonging to a Franciscan convent just up the road. We raise beef and dairy cows, sheep, pigs, poultry, and vegetables. This land produces virtually all our food, *and virtually all our animal feed as well.* In addition, our farm produces all its own fertility. We raise some meat and milk for the convent, and dairy cows to sell. We've done this with little money, with family labor, hand work and simple power tools, and essentially no prior experience. Our most important educational advantage has been that we believed it could be done.

The foundation of this working, sustainable food system is the understanding that good farming cannot be posited upon violations of the nature of Nature. Therefore, we must conclude that permanent groundcovers – grass, pasture – are and should be the default condition for non-wooded land and therefore for land managed for human food production.

Well-managed grasslands create, improve and protect soil, and have diversity with which to respond to virtually any climatic variation. A sound system of food production recognizes and respects that grass is the preferential option for ecological health in non-forested lands; and intensively managed grazing herds are key to ecologically sound grassland management. Pastured animals are foundational to a resilient, renewable human food system.

This is not a new idea. From the beginning, humanity has depended on herbivorous animals for food, therefore on the grasslands that sustain them.

****

A little bit of plant science: Unlike tilled land, which is bare much of the year, perennial pasture harvests sunlight year-round, and with great efficiency. The wide variety of plant species comprising native pasture, with their different leaf shapes, sizes, colors, heights, and angles, means native pasture harvests most of the light falling on it and converts that light to edible plant parts. Grazing triggers root-shed and regrowth, capturing and storing a large portion of that energy in the form of humus.

So grass is central to our family farming practices; and in order that our pastures may provide natural foods for our animals, hence for us, not only today, but in the future, we practice holistic grass management, often called 'rotational grazing'.

The patterns of holistic grazing imitate the migratory grazing patterns of wild herbivores. In a natural setting, where grazing animals are the prey species of large predators, the grass-eaters form large herds for mutual safety. The presence of predators keeps the grazing animals concentrated, so they quickly eat, stomp, or soil the plants underfoot. This forces them to keep moving to fresh ranges; it makes them migratory.

The grasslands that have been grazed, stomped, and manured will regrow before the grazing herds return. Deposits of manure and urine, and the shed roots of the grazed plants, build up humus and fertility in the soil. When the herbivores come back, they find a new abundance of food.

Intensive grass management is a form of biomimicry. In imitation of the natural pattern, the herder of domestic animals keeps his flocks bunched and moving to achieve the same results. Herds and flocks of this kind must be small enough for human-scale management.

The systematic eradication of large predators in North America with the advent of European settlers, and the invention of barbed wire at the end of the 19th century, resulted in a radical shift in animal management practices. Regular, attentive, and consistent human management was no longer deemed necessary. In the absence of predators, and with passive barriers to prevent long-distance migration, the grazing patterns of domestic herds changed dramatically. No longer needing to bunch for safety, cattle spread out, each in search of the best mouthful.

Like children without parental oversight at a buffet, domestic herbivores, relieved of competition for each bite, became more selective. Sweeter and fresher forages got preferential attention; more fibrous or bitter plants were left ungrazed. Once grazed, the favored plants quickly put on fresh shoots, which would be grazed preferentially as well. Frequent, repeated grazing debilitated and then eradicated forage species.

****

Continuously-grazed pastures like these decrease in abundance and fertility over time. This is because repeated grazing without sufficient time for plant recovery kills favored species. Woody and thorny varieties are left ungrazed; eventually these shade out and replace non-woody plants (grass and forbs). Grasslands revert to brush, then woodlands; or, in a brittle environment, they become desert.

Properly-managed periodic grazing, on the other hand, is beneficial to grass and forbs. Top growth is pruned, allowing light to reach new growth points at ground level. Root mass is sloughed in response to top pruning, leaving organic matter to decompose under the soil surface; when soil biota consume the plant material, its energy becomes available for new plant growth. Manure and urine from the grazing animals provides nitrogen for soil fertility.

The object of planned, periodic grazing is to allow extended periods for pasture regrowth and recovery. Before an area is regrazed, pasture plants have time to rebuild their photosynthesizing leaf mass and use it to lay down new energy stores in their roots. They are able to flower and set seed, ensuring subsequent generations of their species.

Holistic grazing offers other benefits. Under continuous grazing, constantly manured soil will have a extended exposure to manure-borne germs and parasites. The long periods of rest in a holistic management system allow time for sunlight, biological activity, and time lapse to eliminate pathogens. Further, increased soil organic matter means increased soil permeability and moisture retention, so that drought and flood resistance are other benefits of holistic grazing. And the expanded diversity of plant species that follows natural grazing patterns provides resilience in various climate situations.

Good pasture management builds diversity and abundance, soil and soil fertility. Management of this kind requires observation and critical decision-making. It is not something that can be scaled up indefinitely. Grass management happens on the human scale.

There can be no overstating the significance that grazing animals have in a non-industrial human food system. Grass is the crop that grows by itself, without any tillage, without a seed being sown; it is the crop that is available in every season; it is the crop on which human survival depends. Only herbivores can give us access to its energy.

****

Animal-sourced foods, our highest quality proteins, fall into two categories, which may be thought of in terms of those which are harvested daily, and the once-and-you're-done harvest.

Dairy animals and egg-laying poultry produce harvestable protein every 12 – 24 hours. Properly cared for, a milk cow can provide milk from grass to feed a family continuously for at least a decade. A laying hen may produce eight hundred or more eggs in her three-to-five-year lifetime. At the end of their productive lives, both can be harvested for meat.

Meat animals provide a single, large protein harvest, once.

Both harvests are appropriate to a biomimetic system; in a human food system, primacy of place goes to the daily, renewable harvest.

Farming of this kind has been the rule in Western cultures for centuries. It is labor-intensive, but not oppressively so. Even today many cultures, as, for example, dairy farmers in the Bavarian Alps, devote considerable time, energy, and attention to intensive grass and herd management. With the invention of temporary portable electric fence, intensive management has come within the reach even of people otherwise thoroughly enmeshed in the industrialized culture. You can have a day job and still manage a flock of sheep, or a herd of cattle or goats.

Grass management is something our whole family has taken part in. Even small children play a role. Young people can take on the bulk of the responsibility for an animal or herd. The time commitment of intensive grass management varies from day to day, but is consistent with ordinary family responsibilities. Our grass harvests most of the energy required by the whole farm, and enables us to produce not only 95% of our own food, but 90% of our animals' food as well.

With portable solar-powered electric fence, we portion off small areas of grass, called 'paddocks'. Our animals are moved to a fresh paddock twice daily, after they are milked.

That milk feeds not only our household, but our pigs and poultry, and our guard and pest control animals – dogs and cats. Such practices were common among all our farming ancestors.

We manage grazing patterns so that pastures are improved by the grazing, fertility is stored in the soil, and more soil is built; this is our provision for the future – our own, our children's, the land's.

Furthermore, we set aside small areas for tillage and grow vegetables for our own use, as well as to feed our omnivorous livestock (pigs and poultry); these we store passively so they feed us all year. We use one unheated hoop house to extend our season of fresh vegetables.

Our staple crop is potatoes; we grow between 1000 and 3000 lb. of potatoes a year. These provide our principle starch. We do buy local wheat, but should our source of wheat dry up, we could provide our carbohydrate needs as potatoes. All our other vegetables and fruits are also grown here. Fertility for the gardens is generated by the farm livestock, particularly the pigs and chickens.

We butcher our own animals, and the offal from each species feeds other domestic animals; chickens feed pigs, pigs feed chickens, cows feed both. Bones go to the dog, or to the compost heap.

All manures are returned to the soil, some directly, some composted and applied to our gardens.

****

Biomimetic farming informs all the patterns of energy flow on the farm. For fuel, it depends on local sunlight, and the local products of that sunlight, especially grass. Grass feeds grazing animals; grazing feeds the soil. Ruminants, as grass-eaters, make solar energy available to us out of forms otherwise inaccessible. They eat what we can't eat, and turn it into milk and meat, which we can.

Historically, poultry and pigs have played another role in human agricultural systems, a role that has been, as must be expected, eminently practical.

Subsistence farming, if it works at all, produces many kinds of surplus calories. Not all the products of agriculture are immediately accessible or desirable for human consumption. Much of what is grown is non-food, plant parts we either cannot eat, or would rather not eat – stems, seeds, peels, cores, rinds, vines, leaves, stalks; overripe, underripe, damaged, moldy.

And much seasonal abundance is *perishable surpluses*, unstable calories that, because they do not have an immediate use, will be lost to spoilage. Fresh fruits and vegetables decay rapidly. Dairying produces an abundance of skim milk, buttermilk, and whey. Butchering results in offal.

Prior to long-distance shipping, refrigeration, and mega-cities, at the time when food production was a local, personal, and all-absorbing priority, the vital job of omnivores in the human food system was the long-term conversion and storage of these sub-par and perishable calories. By feeding unstable and low-quality surpluses to pigs and poultry, humans were able to concentrate valuable proteins and fats in non-perishable, and even self-replicating, forms.

Pigs, especially, excel in this area. Their elastic metabolisms enable them to gorge in times of plenty, then drop to a maintenance ration when food calories are less abundant. They can grow fast, and they can just hang on. And their reproductive capacity – a single sow can produce and raise more than thirty piglets a year – means the inclusion of pigs in human farming enables rapid and radical increases in food storage capacity. Pigs are famine insurance – they convert and store foods during periods of plenty and make those calories available in times of dearth.

The role of omnivores is equally significant for its swift diversion of organic energy from potentially pathogenic decay to immediately useful soil amendment in the form of manure. Instead of putrefaction, we get fertilizer.

Chickens, as the other farm omnivore, share the pig's ability to convert waste into protein, combined with the dairy animal's gift of providing a daily harvest.

The sun shines, grass grows, ruminants eat it; ruminants make milk, meat, and manure; pastures are fertilized. Pigs and chickens eat food surpluses and by-products, and they fertilize gardens, producing more surpluses. Everyone gets fed, humans included.

Biomimetic, human-scale farming works. Some form of it is what has sustained humanity right into the last century or so. It still works.

****

But why bother? The pressure is almost overwhelming to do otherwise. Cash jobs will pay you to specialize in anything from scanning brain waves to scanning UPC symbols. Virtually everything we need or imagine ourselves to need is to be had for money. Everywhere there are corporations ready to provide for our most remote desire by proxy. Food, shelter, clothing, entertainment, health care, child care, education – even acts of charity are dispensed remotely. Air, water, and waste elimination are bought and paid for, leaving us free to ply our specialty for cash. Isn't that good enough?

In answer, two questions come to mind: First, indeed, whether enacting our vocation by proxy can ever be good enough; and secondly, does it work?

The second question begs for priority; the answer to it presses upon us every day, because the answer is NO.

Who would argue that, having contracted with the commercial world to birth, raise, and educate our children, we are enjoying results that are overwhelmingly satisfactory? That the superabundance of food that is to be had anywhere in the country where a Walmart raises its blue-and-gold banner is delicious, or making us healthy? Who would declare that our homes are more homelike, our clothing warmer and more beautiful, our neighborhoods more neighborly, in this world of commercial/industrial provision? No one with an option for something else.

And if the results are *not* satisfying, it should be easy enough to answer the first question: Again, NO. Obviously if the substitutes we have paid for are doing a poor job, something is not right. But even were the results satisfactory, could we ever be justified in turning over our most personal and God-given responsibilities to another person and taking his word that those responsibilities have been fulfilled? What sort of answer can we give ourselves – or God – when asked for a progress report?

Let's look back at chapter one of Genesis, and God's original mandate for His new Creation:

> God blessed them, and God said to them, "Be fruitful and multiply, and fill the earth and subdue it; and have dominion over the fish of the sea and over the birds of the air and over every living thing that moves upon the earth."

"Fill the earth,", "have dominion over the fish… the birds… every living thing that moves on the earth."

Are God's words figurative? Were they just a suggestion for how His new children might put in the time until they came up with technological work-arounds?

For most of history, humanity had to take these words pretty literally, if, that is, we wanted to live. For most of history God's original mandate described the overwhelming focus of our lives. Earth care *was* the human vocation, because if it hadn't been, humanity wouldn't have been around long. When the stakes are extinction or survival, we're motivated. Under these conditions, few people are going to be content to give a sleepy proxy to a distant and impersonal economy to provide for their needs.

But even today, when to the casual observer things might seem to be going well in the economy of specialization; when our chosen avocation will generate ample or at least adequate cash remuneration, and we can afford, financially, to put all our focus into our specialty and use the proceeds to pay others to deal with less worthy matters – like food, shelter, and provision for our family – how certain are we that it is morally acceptable to pay someone else to fulfill our duties? No matter how pricey, slick, or even excellent the substitute, how many of our personal responsibilities are we justified in farming out to someone else?

Motherhood, for example. Pay enough and you can buy your infant a high-class nanny. She's professionally trained, with a medical background; she can handle cloth diapers, diagnose infant maladies, and will speak French to your newborn. The night nurse is careful, attentive, and gentle, always getting up at the least sound from the baby. You can afford to buy human milk from a carefully curated milk bank; it's scrupulously fresh, just thaw and serve. Your baby can rest in caring arms while you make all the money to pay for it practicing law in defense of small businessmen, immigrants, pro-life groups and the environment. Isn't this the best of all possible worlds? Fulfillment for you, civic benefits for everybody else, and the best of everything for your baby?

The answer? NO.

There are some responsibilities that we must simply fulfill in our own persons. Kisses and hugs. Personal presence. Sympathy. Begetting. And if these, what others? Justice? Or may we leave it to another to see that justice is done, and when the results are called into question, say simply 'it wasn't my job, ask him'? Charity, perhaps – how about Matthew 25:40, 'Whatsoever you do'? Can our care for 'the least of my brothers' be justly fulfilled by proxy?

Someone out there – some corporation, or cadre of corporations – is ready and anxious to take the entire question of feeding your family completely – forgive the pun – off your plate. They already have done, in fact. They've seen to virtually every calorie that passes the lips of virtually every American, virtually every day. They've taken over responsibility for producing, processing, packaging, serving size, nutritional content, purity, safety, availability, cooking, refrigerating, shipping, preserving, and dealing with by-products and wastes; almost the only thing left to us to decide is where to buy it, and where to eat it. And, in any case, we're busy with a thousand other things. Not selfish things, but important things – standing on the sidelines cheering at Johnny's soccer game; drilling Jenny on the provinces of Asia for her geography bee; driving Grandma to her hair dressing appointment; putting out fires; saving lives.

Why should we take personal responsibility for our food?

Might it not be sufficient reason, that growing things is the only specific mandate given us by our Creator at the moment of creation? And if this reason is not sufficient, then: Are we satisfied with how it's being done for us? Do the results demonstrate even adequate quality? Are the methods employed ecologically sustainable? Is commercial food provision reliable -- are we confident that those who bring our food to the table do so impartially, will go on doing so just as long as we can pay for it, no other strings attached?

These are serious questions. If you believe that your family's food interests, this matter of life-and-death, are safely in the hands of those who can and will do a better job than you – that they can be counted upon to go on doing that job while leaving your moral choices strictly to your conscience – maybe you don't have to ask these questions.

But there is another point to be made. It's an issue on which many popes have written in recent centuries, initially with great urgency, latterly in a more subdued way, as if by long neglect the ache has dulled, and we are more inclined to accept it as one of the casualties of modern times. That angle might be described as 'the dereliction of the vocation of the family'.

With the shift, since the Industrial Revolution, from man as husbandman, farmer, and provisioner, to man as wage-earner, professional, or entrepreneur, the original nature of Family as blood relatives enacting servanthood for one another has largely been forgotten, nullified in the minds of our grandparents' generation, casting no shadow in our own. This shift, from mutual productivity to joint checking account, leaves us with the name of family, but not its enactment. As Mr. Wendell Berry reminds us, often and urgently, the substance of marriage, of family, of love, is in daily shared labor and the things those labors build. Nothing enacts marriage and family so completely and eloquently as the keeping of family land for producing the family's food now and in the future. Without work, the union is in danger of becoming merely words, a legal document, licit conjugal relations.

The danger of this shift extends not only to the married couple, but to the family as a whole. Service to land, to livestock, and to one another is the breath of our vocation as family. When this is replaced by non-productive cohabitation and a mutually limiting, hence individually competitive, household budget, how is the family to realize itself as, in the words of the Catechism, a 'school of service and sacrifice' (CCC 2224)? While farming may not be the only way for a family to live its vocation, Pope Pius XII was inspired to tell farmers that their 'contact with Mother Earth has a deep social significance', performing 'an *indispensable* function as *source and defense of a stainless moral and religious life*' (*On Rural Life*, 1946; emphasis ours). ' Indispensable'; a big word, a morally demanding word.

Still – so what?

Are we beating a dead horse, invoking an impracticable alternative? Choices that are not choices bear no moral weight, and don't deserve that we should spend much time on them. If the modern economy, complete with its superabundance, its precariousness, and its poor quality, is all there is, then it's the best we can do, and there's an end to it. No one need expect that we'll hang our heads and beat our breasts because we buy our food at Costco.

But *is* this the best the average person can do? *Do* we have options?

We think so. Here are some of our suggestions:

We can make an effort to know where our food is coming from. This almost certainly means beginning a process of weaning ourselves from big box stores. Ninety-five percent of the beef in this country goes through one of four centralized, national meat-processing plants; there is absolutely no way for the consumer to know where, how, or how well that beef was produced. We must patronize local stores that purvey locally-produced, transparently-produced foods.

Try to buy direct from the farmer/grower/producer, and be willing to pay him or her more than you would pay a national chain. Much more, or he/she will not be able to go on growing your food. Enlarge your food budget, and remember that food is medicine. Health is cheaper than sickness, so good food is an investment; and justice requires that we willingly allot to the farmer who grows our food 'an income sufficient to maintain (him) in accordance with (his) dignity and cultural needs' (Pope Pius XII, 1946, *On Rural Life*).

If the idea of budgeting more for your food seems difficult, think again. Where is your food coming from? How much do you know about the ancillary effects of how it is being produced – about the care being taken of the land that produced it, or the wages of the farm workers who tilled that land? To what political purposes are your food dollars being put – what causes, 'rights', or social planning are you funding? And in any case, what *are* all the 'more important things' stretching your budget so that food cannot have a bigger share? Does your iphone really need an update? Can you make your old car last another year before you replace it?

We can take an active role in the production of at least some of our food. Grow a tomato vine; plant chives in a window box. Put a border of lettuce around the porch – and then harvest and eat it. Buy raw meat, whole raw produce, and plain dairy products, and then cook with them. Get to know what food looks like in its natural state.

Don't be satisfied with token efforts. Intellectual commitment to an idea is inadequate by itself. It is easy to remain indoors, applauding the dusty efforts of other people who are putting into practice what we know is necessary but are unwilling to get ourselves dirty for. Our educations and intellectual attainments do not excuse us from labor; when food is scarce, our brilliance will win us not a slice of bread.

Get radical. Waste land is everywhere. There is dirt in the cracks of the sidewalk; leaves pile up and decay against the street curb. The scent of a potted basil plant can transform an inner-city apartment kitchenette. Vacant lots sit idle and gather trash; weedy verges are no-man's-land. Let the landless claim squatters' rights; let them beg, steal, or borrow some small piece of earth.

Or maybe you're one of the fortunate ones with money. You don't need to go shopping for a made farm; you might be paying dearly for someone else's mistakes. Instead, go looking for cheap land in proximity to the community you already depend on. Some real estate, even now, is so poor, damaged, or marginal that the asking price is minimal. And there are sheriff's auctions, where land left on the state's hands can go dirt cheap. Given time, Nature would regenerate this land in any case; with biomimetic methods, we can make it happen faster, and feed ourselves at the same time.

If you already have a house with a yard, you're set, at least for now.

And then there's farming, good farming. Not for profit – oh, no, that's what got us her to begin with. As Father Vincent McNabb truculently observed, 'A farm isn't a place for growing wealthy; it's a place for growing corn.' Let's leave profit out of the question, at least until we are thoroughly satisfied that we know the skill from which we propose to make money, and that won't be for a long time.

Instead, let's practice real, regenerative farming, farming that plans to go on farming as far into the future as we can see and then farther than that, because that's the only kind of farming that honors justice. And if it doesn't make money, it doesn't have to cost money, either; it can save a family a whole lot of money, keep fathers home for more hours, give parents and children important work to do together, and the joy of seeing a complex, difficult, all-encompassing *rightness* in our everyday lives.

On a few acres – G.K.'s three is about right – we can keep a cow, feed a pig, put a few hens to scratch around, garden, plant fruit trees. We need some principles to guide us, but we don't need lessons, we don't need tricks, and we don't need experts; if we're reverent and observant, the nature of Nature is all the instructor we'll need.

We *will* need community – people to share work and experience with, people to be a people with – and this will come about naturally. After all, the need is great, and growing greater. And beauty is attractive.

7

Work and Creativity

Gideon Lazar

Can theology tell us anything about how we should work? Theology often serves to answer our deepest questions, and work is undoubtedly one of the most central aspects of human life.

Scripture opens with God's great work of creation, and its narrative culminates with God's other great work, Christ and the New Creation. Scripture thus invites us to theologize about the meaning of work.

In this brief essay, I want to offer a few thoughts about how theology, and in particular the theology of creation, might better teach us to think about work. In the first section, I look at the model worker, God. In the second section, I turn to the creation of man and his vocation to work. Finally, in the last section, I look at the fact that man is created in the image of God, and so His work ought to mirror God's work.

I. Divine Creativity

The very first thing that the Bible tells us about God is that He is a creator. We see God the Father, the Word, and the Spirit creating all things from nothing. Over the course of the first three days, God takes this formless matter and shapes it into the visible world. Over the course of the next three days, He fills the world with beautiful things.

We can see the beauty in creation every day. We see it in the natural world and in our neighbors. All things that God made have a certain beauty to them. The scriptures liken God to a craftsman, a potter, and many other professions that involve the creation of beauty.

The Psalmists reflected on this beauty in the world more than any other of the authors of scripture. One Psalmist declares that "The heavens are telling the glory of God; and the firmament proclaims His handiwork" (Ps 19:1). Another Psalmist praises God by saying "O Lord, how manifold are Thy works! In wisdom hast Thou made them all" (Ps 104:24). These psalms not only remind us to reflect on the beauty of creation, but that this beauty should lead us back to praising the Creator.

In this life, we do not know God directly, but only "through a glass, darkly" (1 Cor 13:12). In this life we first come to know God "through the things that were made" (Rom 1:20). This means that we come to know God through His creative work!

What does it mean that God is creative? While many pre-Christian philosophers had an idea of an infinite first principle of the universe, and many called this God, none of them understood it as creator. The pagan philosopher Plotinus used the imagery of a glass that contains so much goodness that it ends up overflowing, and this overflow of goodness becomes the universe. Imagine a wine glass that had too much wine poured in it, causing it to overflow and leave a stain on the tablecloth. Could that stain really be called beautiful or creative? It would just be a mistake.

In contrast to this, the Church has always taught that God freely created the world. God is perfect in His infinite Trinitarian life and has no need to create anything outside Himself. However, He is also a personal God with intellect and will, and so can freely create if He chooses. Without freedom, "creation" would just be a necessary overflow. Any beauty would be the result of chance or necessity, not God's goodness. By understanding God as creator, we can now understand the first condition for creativity: ***creativity requires freedom.***

Creation reveals God to us. If God's act of creation is free, how can it still reveal God to us? It could seem that God's act of creation is arbitrary if He did not have to do it. However, true freedom is not arbitrary. To understand how, let us turn to St. Thomas Aquinas's explanation of divine freedom.[1]

St. Thomas Aquinas explains that God could have made anything by His absolute power. Thus, it was genuinely within God's power to do otherwise. When God does create, He does so through His ordered power. That is, God does not use His full power in creating, but only His power as ordered to an end.

Think of a sculptor. A sculptor would first think about the sculpture he wishes to carve. Then, he would figure out what exactly the sculpture should look like. If he wishes to create a sculpture of a baby, he would need to carve the proper proportions for a baby. If he

---

[1] *Summa Theologiae* I, q. 25, a. 5.

carved the head to look like a full grown man, it would not look right on the baby. This does not mean it would have been bad if the sculptor had chosen to carve a full grown man, only that it is not fitting to have the head of a full grown man on a baby given that he chose to carve a baby.

If God had made a different world, he could have made it entirely differently. However, given the way he desired the world to be, there was a certain fittingness to it. For example, if he had made a world without gravity but still required us to need air to breathe, it would have been impossible for life to exist. This would not have been fitting with the end of creating life.

This is why it is important that God not only have will, but also intellect. Without a well-ordered intellect, one does not have true freedom. Consider two people at a piano. The first has never taken a piano lesson, while the other is a master pianist. Both can hit all the same keys. However, only the master pianist is free to play Mozart. There is no physical restriction on the untrained man that keeps him from playing Mozart, but he will not know how to. Even if we give the first man enough lessons to hit all the keys to play the sheet of music, he still will lack the expertise to freely create a new, beautiful piece of music, while the master pianist will be able to.

What was the fitting end that God made all things for? While the Church has never given an official answer to this question, many theologians have speculated that it was for the Incarnation![2] The Incarnation was the greatest work of God, and so it would be most fitting that everything be made for it. God first decided that He would extend Himself outside Himself and would do so by uniting Himself to another nature. God then chose to create a world which it would be fitting to become incarnate in.

God's creative act of making the world then can be thought of as the Father creating a house for His Son. It is an eternal act of love. The Son was already perfect from eternity, but the Father loved Him so much as to create the world for Him.

Understanding God as creator now allows us to understand the second condition for creativity: ***creativity requires a purpose and***

---

[2] For an overview of various scriptural texts and theologians relevant to this topics, see Jean-François Bonnefoy, *Christ and the Cosmos*, trans. Michael D. Meliach, (Paterson: St. Anthony Guild Press, 1965).

fitting structure for that purpose.

Taking together our two requirements for creativity, let us now propose a definition. An act is creative if it is ***done freely with a fitting structure for a certain end.***

II. The Vocation to Work

The creation story in Genesis helps us to understand the fundamental vocations of mankind. In the first creation story, humans are called to "Be fruitful and multiply, and fill the earth and subdue it; and have dominion over the fish of the sea and over the birds of the air and over every living thing that moves upon the earth" (Gen 1:28). In the second creation story, which zooms in on day six, Adam, who in a sense represents all of humanity,[3] is "put him in the garden of Eden to till it and keep it" (Gen 2:15). We see that from the very beginning, man is called to work. For six days God worked, and at the very end of these days God created man to continue on this work.

St. John Paul II, in his encyclical *Laborem exercens*, explores the meaning of the vocation of work in light of these scriptural passages. He distinguishes two aspects of work found in these passages: the objective sense and the subjective sense.[4] The objective sense is that which the person works upon, the object of his work. The subjective sense is the effect that the work has upon the person doing it.

Genesis reveals the object of man's work as the transformation of the creation. When God first makes matter, it is dark, formless, and void. On the first day, God brightens creation with light. On the next two days, God forms the world by dividing Heaven and Earth with the firmament and then dividing land from sea. Starting on the third day and then continuing on for the next three days, God fills the world, placing stars and planets in the firmament, birds in the sky, fish in the sea, and plants, and humans on the land. God has taken formless matter and made it into something beautiful. Man's call to subdue the earth continues this process. As St. John Paul II says,

---

[3] This is not to say that Adam was *not* a historical figure, but that as the head of the human family, Adam also stands as our representative.

[4] St. John Paul II is using *obiectum* and *subiectum* in the older, scholastic meaning of these words. The subject is the one acting, and the object is the thing being acted upon, like the subject and object of a sentence. Objective here does not mean "more real" than the subjective.

This universality and, at the same time, this multiplicity of the process of "subduing the earth" throw light upon human work, because man's dominion over the earth is achieved in and by means of work. There thus emerges the meaning of work in an objective sense, which finds expression in the various epochs of culture and civilization. Man dominates the earth by the very fact of domesticating animals, rearing them and obtaining from them the food and clothing he needs, and by the fact of being able to extract various natural resources from the earth and the seas. But man "subdues the earth" much more when he begins to cultivate it and then to transform its products, adapting them to his own use.[5]

The language of "subdue" and "dominion" is language that is ordinarily used of a king in the Bible. Man is king over creation. When we work, we exercise our kingship by transforming the natural resources of the world into something new.

Adam's vocation in the garden sheds greater light upon this. Biblical scholars have pointed out that both Genesis 1 and 2 describe the creation of the world as a temple. Genesis 1 has the world created in seven steps, just as the tabernacle in Exodus is given by God in seven speeches, or how Solomon's temple is constructed in seven years.[6] At the end of the week, God comes and rests on the Earth, just as how in ancient temples the god would come to rest in the temple after its construction.[7] In Genesis 2, Eden, the garden, and the world correspond to the Holy of Holies, the Holy Place, and the Courtyard in the later tabernacle and temples of Israel.[8] Adam then is placed in the Garden as a priest. Ezekiel even describes Adam using the language of the high priest of Israel (Eze 28:13). In fact, the Hebrew words for "to till and to keep," *abad* and *shamar*, are words later used

---

[5] *Laborem exercens* 5.

[6] Ratzinger, *The Spirit of the Liturgy*, trans. John Saward, (San Francisco: Ignatius Press, 2000), 26-27; Peter J. Kearney, "Creation and Liturgy: The P Redaction of Ex 25—40," *Zeitschrift für die alttestamentliche Wissenschaft* 89, no. 3 (1977): 375-387.

[7] John H. Walton, *The Lost World of Genesis One: Ancient Cosmology and the Origins Debate*, (Downers Grove: InterVarsity Press, 2009).

[8] Ephrem the Syrian, *Hymns on Paradise*, trans. Sebastian Brock, (Crestwood: SVS Press, 1990); Matthias Joseph Scheeben, *Handbook of Catholic Dogmatics*, trans. Michael J. Miller, (Steubenville: Emmaus Academics, 2021), n. 1429; Steven C. Smith, *The House of the Lord: A Catholic Biblical Theology of God's Temple Presence in the Old and New Testaments*, (Steubenville: Franciscan University Press, 2017).

to describe the liturgical work of the priests in the temple.[9] Man's vocation of work is part of his call to be a priest. Adam ministers to God as a priest by working in the garden.

Man's call to exercise his dominion in a priestly way makes clear that his dominion is not to be abused. Pope Francis has pointed out that the fall has distorted our proper dominion over the earth.[10] Our call to serve God through dominion frequently becomes distorted into tyranny. What then is the proper way in which we should work? First, we must ensure our work is ordered towards the growth of the kingdom of God. We see this again in Genesis 2. Four rivers flow out of the garden into the world, and various precious metals and stones are said to be in these lands. At the end of the book of Revelation, we see that the garden has now become a garden-city, and the various metals and stones are part of the city. Man through his work has gone out to the end of the earth and brought the resources of the world into the garden, transforming them and building up God's kingdom. All our work must be oriented towards the building up of this kingdom, which is the Church.

Secondly, we must ensure our work is ordered towards the good of the workers. This reveals the subjective sense of work spoken of earlier. If man's fundamental vocation is to work, then work must serve the good of man. St. John Paul II explains that,

> Man has to subdue the earth and dominate it, because as the "image of God" he is a person, that is to say, a subjective being capable of acting in a planned and rational way, capable of deciding about himself, and with a tendency to self-realization. As a person, man is therefore the subject of work... And so this "dominion" spoken of in the biblical text being meditated upon here refers not only to the objective dimension of work but at the same time introduces us to an understanding of its subjective dimension. Understood as a process whereby man and the human race subdue the earth, work corresponds to this basic biblical concept only when throughout the process man manifests himself and confirms himself as the one who "dominates"... In fact there is no doubt that human work has an ethical value of its own, which clearly and directly remains linked to the fact that the one who carries it out is a person, a conscious and free subject, that is to say a subject that decides about himself... In fact, in the final analysis it is always man who is the

---

[9] G. K. Beale, *The Temple and God's Mission: A Biblical Theology of the Dwelling Place of God*, (Downers Grove: InterVarsity Press, 2004), 66-77.
[10] Pope Francis, *Laudato si'* 66.

purpose of the work, whatever work it is that is done by man-even if the common scale of values rates it as the merest "service," as the most monotonous even the most alienating work.[11]

We must always consider the good of the worker when discussing work. In the ancient world, pagan cultures saw work as slavery. The common people were enslaved to kings and gods and worked for them, even in the afterlife, with no hope of anything better. In contrast, the Bible sees work as something man does along with God. Work is always ordered towards rest in the Bible, both the weekly sabbatical rest and the eternal rest in Heaven. In fact, when God becomes man, he spends the majority of his earthly life as a humble worker. Although work has become toilsome, this too is for our sake, to help remedy the distortion of dominion from the fall.[12] Through our struggles in work, we are able to offer these sufferings up to God to help build virtue and sanctify our souls.

III. Creativity and the Image of God

So far we have explored God's creative work and man's work in creation. Right in between these two themes is a key verse: "Then God said, "Let us make man in our image, after our likeness" (Gen 1:26). Man's work is premised upon being made in the image of God. Since God's work is creative, man's work must also be creative!

What makes man's work creative? Earlier, we defined a creative act as one which is done freely with a fitting structure for a certain end. If man's work is truly creative, it must meet each of these requirements.

Man's work is free because man has free will. Pre-Christian philosophers did not conceive of free will. For example, in Plato's dialogue the *Gorgias*, Socrates thinks the only reason people act immorally is because of an intellectual error. Either they must be educated on what is good or they are just too stupid to understand morality. The Christian faith rejected this understanding of free will. St. Paul says, "I do not understand my own actions. For I do not do what I want, but I do the very thing I hate" (Rom 7:15). Just because one knows what is good does not mean one will do it. Especially in this fallen state, man is weighed down by sin, which causes him to

---

[11] *Laborem exercens* 6.
[12] *Laborem exercens* 9.

choose evil. However, even once restored by grace, man is free to choose or reject God. The great Old Testament teacher Sirach says that God "created man in the beginning, and he left him in the power of his own inclination. If you will, you can keep the commandments, and to act faithfully is a matter of your own choice" (Sir 15:14-15).

Man, made in the image of a creative God, is free to choose. This should not be reduced though to the freedom to choose between good and evil. God cannot choose evil, but this does not mean that God is not free. Rather, our freedom, like God's freedom, finds its fullest realization in the freedom to choose between multiple goods.

Man's work must be directed towards the building up of the kingdom of God. We see in Revelation that the age to come is a garden-city. There is a mixture of the natural world, created by God, and a city, which is built by man. Man cooperates with God's grace to build up the kingdom. However, God's grace does not destroy human freedom, for grace does not destroy nature, but perfects it. God's grace frees humans from sin and allows them to freely choose between many goods. This means the kingdom of God has many creative contributions from humans. The creative work of a Christian is directed towards the ultimate end, Christ and his kingdom.

Finally, since grace perfects nature, growth in grace and virtue allows each person to contribute his unique gift to the Church. Since each person exercises creativity, each person is able to offer his creative contribution in a fitting way.

Of all the creatures of the Earth, humans alone can work creatively, since humans have an intellect and a will. By his intellect, a man can create in a fitting way. By his will, he can freely and creatively create. This is an essential aspect of the image of God.

The freedom of the will is especially important for creativity in our current day. The development of artificial intelligence has raised significant questions in the world of business. Could AI replace all human work? While AI may replace many parts of human work, they cannot replace creativity.

Blessed John Duns Scotus brings in an important philosophical distinction to understand why. Drawing on Aristotle and St. John of Damascus, Scotus distinguishes between natural powers and rational (i.e. voluntary) powers.[13] Natural powers necessarily (or randomly) move to their end, while rational powers are able to choose between alternatives. Since all the components of computers are natural, there is nothing with AI that allows it to be truly rational. Only man, endowed with free will, can be rational. AI can do things that would require high intelligence for a human to do, but at the end of the day, they can only follow their programing. Even when they have been trained using machine learning, the "learning" method is simply generating an algorithm more complex than a human could ever understand. This is not the creation of rationality.

This means that the best AI can do is the powers given to it by humans. When encountering a genuinely new problem, it will be unable to be creative. Furthermore, it will not have the stamp of human creativity in its work, and so will not reflect the true value found within human creative works. Even if it can be hard from the outside to distinguish AI generated art and true human art, human freedom creates a genuine difference in value between the two.

In his essay *On Fairy Stories*, JRR Tolkien considers the work of "subcreation" to be an essential aspect of the image of God. Just as God created this world, so too humans are called to create their own miniature worlds. When we work, we continue after the pattern of God's creativity. We do not create *ex nihilo* like God does, but rather we learn from His creativity. We are not independent creators, but subcreators, freely acting within the larger framework of divine providence.[14] As St. Thomas Aquinas says,

> art imitates nature. The reason for this is that, as principles are related to each other, so proportionally are their works and effects related. Now the principle of those things that come to be from art is the human intellect, which is derived, after a sort of likeness, from the divine intellect, the principle of natural objects. From this, it is necessary both that art's work imitate nature's work, and that those things which exist by art imitate those which exist in nature. For if some instructor of some art were to effect some work of art, it would be necessary for the student, who takes up his art from it, to attend to the instructor's work, so that according to its likeness he might himself also work. And therefore, the human

---

[13] *Questions on the Metaphysics of Aristotle*, bk. 9, q. 15. This distinction is found, although to a lesser extent, in St. Thomas Aquinas as well.

[14] For more on the relation of divine providence and freedom, see another essay of mine in this volume, "God Works All Things for Good: The Role of the Devil in Divine Providence and the Permission of Evil."

intellect—whose intelligible light is derived from the divine intellect—necessarily has to be informed, in those things that it makes, by looking into those things that are naturally made, so that it might work similarly.[15]

We learn from the great Creator and then we create in His image.

For Tolkien, this subcreativity was the creation of Middle Earth. However, one does not need to be an author to exercise creativity. Tolkien's lesson here is universal. Any worker is a subcreator. Everyone does things in a slightly different way, and in this way, they bring their own creativity. Of course, this creativity needs to be ordered to its proper end. Creativity always ought to be well-ordered, just as God's willing is well-ordered. This is the role of a boss at a company, who can direct all things towards the objective end of any work. However, we must also always remember the subjective end of any work, the good of the people doing it. In divine providence, God is able to use our free actions towards His ultimate goal, the building up of the Church of Jesus Christ. Perhaps we can learn from how God uses freedom and creativity in His own work to better learn how to integrate it into ours.

---

[15] Thomas Aquinas, *Commentary on the Politics*, trans. Richard J. Regan, (Indianapolis: Hackett Publishing, 2007), prologue.

Part III: Contemplating the Creator

8

Earth, Water, & Fire: Three Classical Elements of Desert Spirituality

David Valerio

I. Introduction

My book, sir philosopher, is the nature of created things, and it is always at hand when I wish to read the words of God.[1]

Stereotypically, the monastic life is perceived as entailing a rejection of the world. In this view, the select men and women who left society in order to enter the wilderness did so in order to save their own souls, unencumbered by temptations from interactions with other created beings. While there is some truth to this, it doesn't imply that the Desert Monastics detested Creation. In fact, the spirituality of the desert was marked by a profound reverence for Earth. It was embodied, practical, and deeply concerned with the monk's harmonious relationship with the natural world. To partake in the divine nature and enter into union with God, the monk had to commune with the created world that God made and sustains. How can one love the Creator without loving His Creation, which He saw and called "very good" (Gen 1:31)?

Numerous stories from these spiritual trailblazers attest to their deep connection to and love for the desert they called home. These accounts describe various interactions between monks and the natural world, reflecting how their chosen environment, with its unique environmental conditions, shaped the way that desert spirituality evolved and came to be practiced. This paper proposes to catalog key ecospiritual learnings from Desert Monastic theory and practice by meditating on sayings from the Fathers and Mothers that explore the ascetical-mystical significance of three classical elements — earth, water, and fire. We have much to learn from these ancient Christians who inhabited the wildest of places, and their example can serve as a model for us moderns to come closer to God and live in greater harmony with the world we are intertwined with.

---

[1] Evagrius, *The Praktikos & Chapters on Prayer*, (Piffard: Cistercian Publications, 1972), 92.

II. Earth

II.1 Work and Reeds

The Desert Monastics placed a high value on physical work as a means of drawing closer to God. If the ascetic did not work, his *nous* would stray from contemplation of God and fall prey to demonic temptations. Engaging in simple manual labor occupied the body, calmed the mind, and provided the monk with a humble means of sustenance. The goal of such manual labor was not the physical fruit that it bore, but rather the inner stillness it fostered. A quintessential example is found at the beginning of the Alphabetical Collection of the Sayings of the Desert Fathers where St. Anthony asked God what he needed to do in order to be saved. God gave him a vision of "a man like himself sitting at his work, getting up from his work to pray, then sitting down and plaiting a rope, then getting up again to pray". An angel then told him that if he did this, then he would be saved.[2] The rhythm of prayer and work repeated in perpetuity was the foundation of salvation to the earliest Christian monastics. Indeed, work was so integral to the spiritual life that to be deprived of it was considered to be a loss:

> There was a blind elder at Skete in the lavra of Abba Sisoes; his cell was located about half a mile from the well. He would never allow anyone else to fetch water for him. He made a rope and attached one end of it to the well, the other to his cell; the rope lay on the ground. When he went to fetch water, he walked along the rope. The elder did this so that he could find the well that way. When the wind blew the sand so that it covered the rope, he would take it up in his hand, shake it and put it back down on the ground and walk along it. When a brother offered to fetch water for him, the elder replied: 'Truly brother, for twenty-two years I have fetched my own water; so you wish to deprive me of my labour?'[3]

What would have been perceived as a generous act by a layman was seen as a slight by the monk. Work was a non-negotiable aspect of monastic life. If one did not work, neither would one eat, either physically or spiritually (2 Thess 3:10).

A recurring theme throughout the early monastic literature is the confrontation between orthodox Christianity and the Euchite, or

---

[2] Benedicta Ward, *The Sayings of the Desert Fathers: The Alphabetical Collection*, (Woonsocket: Mowbray, 1981), para. Anthony the Great 1.

[3] John Moschos, *The Spiritual Meadow*, (Piscataway: Gorgias Press, 2010), ch. 169.

Messalian, heresy ("Messalians").[4] The Euchites rejected the spiritual importance of the sacraments, despised physical disciplines, and believed that prayer alone was necessary for salvation. The Desert Monastics rejected this disembodied philosophy as being utterly antithetical to Christian spirituality. A prime example of this is the story of Abba Lucius' encounter with a band of Euchites. When he asked them what their manual work was, they responded that they had none. Rather, they preferred to "pray without ceasing". Abba Lucius then proceeded to ask them who prayed for them while they were sleeping and received no response. He then said:

> Forgive me, but you do not act as you speak. I will show you how, while doing my manual work, I pray without interruption. I sit down with God, soaking my reeds and plaiting my ropes, and I say, 'God, have mercy on me; according to your great goodness and according to the multitude of your mercies, save me from my sins.'[5]

With the money obtained by this work, he was able to pay others to pray on his behalf while he was sleeping and thus fulfill the commandment. This story shows how ridiculous the denial of material creation as evil was to the orthodox Christian ascetic. Naïve spiritualism had no place in the desert. The human person is a body-soul composite and must strive for salvation in a manner that reflects this reality.

What valuable work could be conducted without the raw materials necessary to fashion cloth, rope, or baskets from? The most important natural resource the monks used to produce these goods were the papyrus sedges, common reeds, aquatic bulrushes, and sea rushes that grew along the riverine distributaries and terrestrial wetlands of the Nile Delta.[6] The role of aquatic vegetation in the monastic way of life is shown by the story of "a great elder [that] came to the river and, finding a placid reed bed, settled there". From this home base, he cut shoots from the reed bed and braided them into ropes, which he then

---

[4] "Messalians," *Catholic Encyclopedia,*
https://www.newadvent.org/cathen/10212a.htm.

[5] Ward, para. Lucius 1.

[6] "Nile Delta Flooded Savanna," *Wikipedia,* accessed July 6 2023, https://en.wikipedia.org/w/index.php?title=Nile_Delta_flooded_savanna&oldid=116 3710940; Lisa-Maria Rebelo and Matthew P. McCartney, "Wetlands of the Nile Basin: Distribution, function, and contributions to livelihoods," in *The Nile River Basin: Water, Agriculture, Governance, and Livelihoods,* (Abingdon: Routledge, 2012), 212-228, International Water Management Institute,
https://www.iwmi.cgiar.org/Publications/Books/PDF/H045318.pdf.

proceeded to throw into the river. We are told that "he did not work because he needed to but for the toil and for hesychia."[7] This account is ambivalent with respect to the loving stewardship of nature, as the way he negligently disposed of his work products in the river shows how the desert Christian could negatively impact the natural world around him through his pursuit of holiness.[8] Nonetheless, it emphasizes that without the natural capital found in his surrounding environment, the monk could not conduct his work for God.

II.2 Love and Geography

The physical environment that the monks chose to make their homes in had a deep spiritual impact on their practice of the Christian faith. There is a reason that they are known to history as the Desert Monastics, since their encounter with the barren landscapes of the arid Near East was reflected in their equally lean, harsh spirituality.[9] The grand vistas to be seen in these "wastelands" lifted the monk's mind and heart up to meditate on the transcendent mysteries of our ineffable, invisible, incomprehensible God. The isolation found in these places unfit for civilization allowed the monk to commune in an intimate way with our Lord, God, and Savior Jesus Christ, without the distractions of the human world to entice them away from the mystical path of *theosis*. The biosphere even warned the monks about spiritual dangers that might arise and how to escape them: "When you see a cell built close to the marsh, know that the devastation of Scetis is near; when you see trees, know that it is at the doors; and when you see young children, take up your sheep-skins, and go away."[10]

A common trope about early Christian monasticism is that it reflects a Gnostic hatred for the created world. This is far from the case. We are told that when St. Anthony first approached his Inner Mountain:

> He came to a very lofty mountain, and at the foot of the mountain ran a clear spring, whose waters were sweet and very cold; outside there was a plain and a few uncared-for palm trees. Antony then, as it were, moved

---

[7] John Wortley, *The Book of the Elders: Sayings of the Desert Fathers; The Systematic Collection*, (Collegeville: Liturgical Press, 2012), 22.

[8] Rachel Wheeler, "The Revelatory Tide: Desert Spirituality and Contemporary Water Crises" *Spiritus: A Journal of Christian Spirituality* 20, no. 2 (2020): 176–93, at 183.

[9] Belden C. Lane, "Desert Catechesis: The Landscape and Theology of Early Christian Monasticism," *Anglican Theological Review* 75, no. 3 (1993): 292–314.

[10] Ward, para. Macarius the Great 5.

by God, loved the place, for this was the spot which he who had spoken with him by the banks of the river had pointed out.[11]

Far from despising the place that he had been called to live in, he saw the beauty of the mountain, with its flowing waters and isolated palms, and instantly fell in love with it. Love is the key word here. The Lord reminds us that the first and greatest commandment is to "love the Lord thy God with thy whole heart, and with thy whole soul, and with thy whole mind", and that the second, "thou shalt love thy neighbor as thyself", is intimately bound up with the first (Matt 22:37-39). What does it mean to love a place? We have a good idea of what love in action looks like when the object is a human person. Sacred Scripture and Holy Tradition contain innumerable examples of how the love of man for his fellow man is an icon of the inner life of the Holy Trinity, who is love incarnate and in essence. Love for one's ecosystem is less clear but nonetheless can be explored through the use of analogy. The fact that after St. Anthony made his home there, he "found a small plot of suitable ground, tilled it; and having a plentiful supply of water for watering" sowed it indicates that love for Creation entails working it into something more fecund than it is by nature alone.[12] Abba John the Eunuch lets us know what love for a place does not look like when he tells his disciples, "My sons, let us not make this place dirty, since our Fathers cleansed it from the demons."[13] Love for the environment was central to Desert Monastic spirituality, but the way it was expressed was specific to particular geographies, analogous to how their sayings on human relationships are specific to the particular people involved.

III. Water

III.1 Thirst and Trust in God

The deserts of Egypt, Syria, Palestine, and Cappadocia are very dry places. The Nitrian Desert of Egypt, a subregion of the larger Western Desert where the early monastic centers of Scetis, Kellia, and Nitria were located, receives on average less than two tenths of an inch of precipitation annually and can go half-centuries or more without

---

[11] Athanasius, "Life of Antony," in *The Complete Ante-Nicene & Nicene and Post-Nicene Church Fathers Collection*, ed. Philip Schaff, (London: Catholic Way Publishing, 2014), para. 49.

[12] Athanasius, para. 50.

[13] Ward, para. John the Eunuch 5.

receiving any rainfall whatsoever.[14] Water is necessary for life. The typical human being can go seven days without drinking water, but in the extreme environments of the earliest monastics this could be as short as seven hours due to the sweltering conditions they encountered and the strenuous walking they often undertook.[15] With this context, one is better equipped to understand just how perilous a situation St. Macarius the Great found himself in when "the water he was carrying [during a twenty-day journey] was exhausted" and was thus in great distress. He was at the point of collapse when a maiden appeared to him "holding a dripping bottle of water and standing about a furlong away from him". This was a mirage that he pursued for three days, and "after her a herd of buffalo appeared to him; a female with a young one came to a halt. Her udder was flowing with milk. He got beneath her and was relieved by sucking her. The buffalo came as far as his cell, suckling him while not letting her calf near her."[16] This story underscores how God will provide drink to those who thirst for Him, sometimes through the intercession of His creatures (Ps 62:2-3). This was also the case when St. Sabas prayed to God for the relief of a little water in the early days after the foundation of the Great Lavra, subsequently seeing "a wild ass digging deep into the earth with its hooves; when it had dug a large hole, he saw it lowering its mouth to the hole and drinking". He was then able to find an unceasing source of flowing water for his monks to drink from going forward.[17]

These accounts of God providing for his servants' thirst foreground the weighty spiritual reality that "not in bread alone doth man live, but in every word that proceedeth from the mouth of God (Matt 4:4). We can do nothing without the Lord. When we try to rely on ourselves, we deny God's omnipotence, omniscience, and omnipresence:

> Abba Doulas, the disciple of Abba Bessarion said, 'One day when we were walking beside the sea I was thirsty and I said to Abba Bessarion,

---

[14] Martin Williams, "West of the Nile: The Western Desert of Egypt and the Eastern Sahara – Part 1," in *The Nile Basin: Quaternary Geology, Geomorphology and Prehistoric Environments*, (Cambridge: Cambridge University Press, 2019), 211–26.
[15] Claude A. Piantadosi, "Water and Salt," in *The Biology of Human Survival: Life and Death in Extreme Environments*, ed. Claude A Piantadosi, (Oxford: Oxford University Press, 2003), 52-53
[16] Palladius, *The Lausiac History*, (Piffard: Cistercian Publications, 2015), para. Macarius of Alexandria 8-9.
[17] Cyril of Scythopolis, *The Lives of the Monks of Palestine*, (Piffard: Cistercian Publications, 1991), 17.

"Father, I am very thirsty." He said a prayer and said to me, "Drink some of the sea water." The water proved sweet when I drank some. I even poured some into a leather bottle for fear of being thirsty later on. Seeing this, the old man asked me why I was taking some. I said to him, 'Forgive me, it is for fear of being thirsty later on.' Then the old man said, 'God is here, God is everywhere.'[18]

Living in a brutal, alien environment had a way of shocking the monks out of their remnant belief in the myth of self-sufficiency. How could he foolishly choose to rely on himself when he saw how quickly he would perish without the Lord to preserve him? This does not mean that the monk could just freeload off God's grace to survive in the desert. He had to constantly beseech the Lord's great mercy in order to endure. One time Abba Moses was planning to make a long trip and wondered how he would be able to find the water he needed to get there. A voice told him, "Go, and do not be anxious about anything." He ended up using his small bottle of water to cook food for some visiting monks, so he argued with God, saying, "You brought me here and now I have no water for your servants", until God sent them some water.[19] The monk must pray with all his heart, mind, and soul lest he not be heard by the Lord. One time some monks who came to Abba Xoius complained about their distress due to a lack of rain. He recommended that they pray. They replied that they said litanies and still it did not rain. Abba Xoius told them that the reason it did not rain is because they did not pray with intensity, and asked if they wanted to see whether he was right. To show them, he "stretched his hands towards heaven in prayer and immediately it rained."[20] One must "ask, and it shall be given you: seek, and you shall find: knock, and it shall be opened to you" with faith, hope, and charity. "For every one that asketh, receiveth: and he that seeketh, findeth: and to him that knocketh, it shall be opened." (v. Matt 7:7-8)

III.2 Erosion and Spiritual Growth

Water works slowly. Many of the most beautiful vistas we find on our planet — the glorious ravines of Zion National Park, the brilliant badlands of North and South Dakota, the magnificent Mississippi River birdfoot delta — were shaped by weathering and erosion,

---

[18] Ward, para. Bessarion 1.
[19] Ward, para. Moses 13.
[20] Ward, para. Xoius 2.

geologic processes set in motion by that most elegant of molecules, H_2O.[21] Yet, water is so widespread as to be ignored (in many places at least). How could such an everyday liquid be so necessary to the existence of life itself, as well as pivotal in shaping the very face of the Earth? The Desert Monastics pointed to the patient, long-suffering work of water as a symbol of how the monk should be while progressing in spiritual life. This can be seen in this story about Abba John the Dwarf:

> It was said of Abba John the Dwarf that he withdrew and lived in the desert at Scetis with an old man of Thebes. His abba, taking a piece of dry wood, planted it and said to him, 'Water it every day with a bottle of water, until it bears fruit.' Now the water was so far away that he had to leave in the evening and return the following morning. At the end of three years the wood came to life and bore fruit. Then the old man took some of the fruit and carried it to the church saying to the brethren, 'Take and eat the fruit of obedience.'[22]

One cannot expect to achieve Christian perfection in a matter of days, months, or years. Final flourishing in the life in Christ is a process that unfolds over the course of one's whole life, on the timescale of decades. We must continue to water our spirit with the practices of prayer, fasting, and almsgiving so that the Lord will grant us the grace to grow as the mustard seed, "which is the least indeed of all seeds; but when it is grown up, it is greater than all herbs, and becometh a tree, so that the birds of the air come, and dwell in the branches thereof" (Matt 13:31).

Water drips. We see this happen often at our kitchen faucets, when they have a worn-out washer or a loose o-ring. It's annoying when this occurs. Yet, these slow dribbles can also produce marvels. One need only see the stalagmites and stalactites of the Carlsbad Caverns of New Mexico to grasp the wonder-working power of slow splashes of water over long periods of time.[23] Abba Moses once used this

---

[21] "Geology - Zion National Park," *U.S. National Park Service,* https://www.nps.gov/zion/learn/nature/geology.htm; "Geologic Formations - How Badlands Buttes Came to Be," *U.S. National Park Service,* https://www.nps.gov/articles/000/badl-geologic-formations.htm; "How Was the Mississippi River Delta Formed?" *Loyola University Center for Environmental Communication,* https://lucec.loyno.edu/how-was-mississippi-river-delta-formed.
[22] Ward, para. John the Dwarf 1.
[23] "Geology Of Carlsbad Caverns National Park," *U.S. Geological Survey,* https://www.usgs.gov/index.php/geology-and-ecology-of-national-parks/geology-carlsbad-caverns-national-park.

hydrologic process to point out the hypocrisy of his fellow monks, in the understated way characteristic of the Desert Monastics:

> A brother at Scetis committed a fault. A council was called to which Abba Moses was invited, but he refused to go to it. Then the priest sent someone to say to him, 'Come, for everyone is waiting for you.' So he got up and went. He took a leaking jug, filled it with water and carried it with him. The others came out to meet him and said to him, 'What is this, Father?' The old man said to them, 'My sins run out behind me, and I do not see them, and today I am coming to judge the errors of another.' When they heard that they said no more to the brother but forgave him.[24]

The protracted, inconspicuous loss of water from the jug emphasizes how cunning the Devil can be when dragging us down from the spiritual heights we are called to. How easy it is to "seest the mote that is in [our] brother's eye; and seest not the beam that is in [our] own eye" (Matt 7:3)! The small sins that we fail to notice build up over time, and eventually lead to dramatic spiritual falls.

Abba Poemen once said that "the nature of water is soft, that of stone is hard; but if a bottle is hung above the stone, allowing the water to fall drop by drop, it wears away the stone. So it is with the word of God; it is soft and our heart is hard, but the man who hears the word of God often, opens his heart to the fear of God."[25] These beautiful lines call attention to the necessity of consistency in spiritual life. To constantly have the Word of God in our mind, on our lips, and in our heart is to always have God before our eyes, as St. Anthony enjoins us to do.[26] In doing this, we allow the Lord to excise our evil habits and leave Jesus Christ to iconographically shine through in the way we live. Lao Tzu, the semi-legendary ancient Chinese philosopher and composer of the Tao Te Ching, notes this perennial truth about the portentous potentialities of water when he states: "Nothing in the world is as soft, as weak, as water; nothing else can wear away the hard, the strong, and remain unaltered. Soft overcomes hard, weak overcomes strong. Everybody knows it, nobody uses the knowledge."[27] The dichotomies, paradoxes, and inversions emblematic of Taoism are also core to Eastern Christianity.[28] St. Paul

---

[24] Ward, para. Moses 2.

[25] Ward, para. Poemen 183.

[26] Ward, para. Anthony the Great 3.

[27] Lao Tzu, *Lao Tzu: Tao Te Ching: A Book about the Way and the Power of the Way*, trans. Ursula K. Le Guin, (Boulder: Shambhala, 1998), ch 78.

[28] Hieromonk Damascene, *Christ the Eternal Tao*, (Valaam Books, 1999).

tells us that when we are weak, then we are powerful (2 Cor 12:10). The Lord tells us that "whosoever shall exalt himself shall be humbled: and he that shall humble himself shall be exalted" (Matt 12:12). The Desert Monastics willingly flowed to the lowest place in their social landscape. They were content to live in caves and holes in the ground, to subsist off bread and foraged vegetation, to pray and work the most mundane tasks. They made fools of themselves for Christ's sake, and in so doing received their crowns of righteousness (1 Cor 4:10, 2 Tim 4:8).

IV. Fire

IV.1 All Flame

God appeared to Moses as a fire writhing within an incombustible burning bush (Exo 3:22). The Holy Spirit descended upon each of the Apostles at Pentecost as tongues of fire (Acts 2:3). St. Paul says that our God is a consuming fire (Heb 12:29). Abba Joseph once said, "You cannot be a monk unless you become like a consuming fire."[29] For the monk to become all flame was for him to become like God. Fire is not a static object, it is a dynamic process. Fire is never the same. It constantly expands and contracts as it interacts with the biogeochemistry of the surrounding environment. It transforms solid matter into ephemeral gas. In a sense, it relates to the outside world in a similar way to how the three persons of the Holy Trinity relate to one another. Fire is a communion of elements. The idea of the monk being like fire is related to Abba Bessarion's statement: "The monk ought to be as the Cherubim and the Seraphim: all eye."[30] The monk must constantly be vigilant; he need always be on watch. He must unceasingly commune with the Father, Son, and Holy Spirit. The following image of the venerable Abba Arsenius, one of the most widely respected of the early Egyptian ascetics, shows us how fire was an icon of the true Desert Monastic:

A brother came to the cell of Abba Arsenius at Scetis. Waiting outside the door he saw the old man entirely like a flame. (The brother was worthy of this sight.) When he knocked, the old man came out and saw the brother marvelling. He said to him, 'Have you been knocking long? Did you see anything here?' The other answered, 'No.' So then he talked

---

[29] Ward, para. Joseph of Panephysis 6.
[30] Ward, para. Bessarion 11.

with him and sent him away.[31]

We also have this remarkable saying from Abba Joseph to ponder as we consider the significance of fire to the spiritual life of the desert:

> Abba Lot went to see Abba Joseph and said to him, 'Abba, as far as I can I say my little office, I fast a little, I pray and meditate, I live in peace and as far as I can, I purify my thoughts. What else can I do?' Then the old man stood up and stretched his hands towards heaven. His fingers became like ten lamps of fire and he said to him, 'If you will, you can become all flame.'[32]

The monk was to conform himself to God in the present moment, at all times, and in all places. He was not to think about the past or future, but rather live out the commandments in the here and now by dying to self. Fire does not self-reflect. It simply acts. It simply is. The *logismoi* cannot touch the monk who is on fire with the Lord, since the demons cannot take him away from the ever-present now. To become all flame is to be fully before the face of God and to be transfigured by Him. Ultimately, fire is a mystery as the Trinity is mysterious. We can explain how it emerges, grows, and persists in as many ways as we like, applying both cataphatic and apophatic knowledge, but the conclusion of our reasoning will lead us back to where we started. What does it mean to be all flame? Who knows. Only God does.

IV.2 Refining Fire and Uncreated Light

Being cleansed of our sins is hard. We would like to be good, but as St. Paul says: "For the good which I will, I do not; but the evil which I will not, that I do. Now if I do that which I will not, it is no more I that do it, but sin that dwelleth in me." (Rom 7:19-20) The demons must be cleared out of us. The Desert Monastics knew this very well from their eternal battles with them in the heart of the desert. Yet this process of purification is often painful. The Lord refines us as fire burns away the imperfections of silver and gold (Prov 17:3). To be thrown into the blazing flames and have our vices incinerated involves many trials and much suffering, but ultimately we come out the better for it. Amma Syncletica spoke to this fact when she said:

> In the beginning there are a great many battles and a good deal of suffering for those who are advancing towards God and afterwards, ineffable joy. It is like those who wish to light a fire; at first they are

---

[31] Ward, para. Arsenius 27.
[32] Ward, para. Joseph of Panephysis 7.

choked by the smoke and cry, and by this means obtain what they seek (as it is said: "Our God is a consuming fire"): so we also must kindle the divine fire in ourselves through tears and hard work.[33]

If we make it through the smoke first kicked up in our attempts to kindle the divine fire of the Holy Spirit within us, we will soon nurture an overpowering internal inferno that scorches our sins so quickly that the fumes do not even have time to rise. We must become so burning hot through embodying heroic virtue that our enemies cannot get anywhere near us. As soon as evil thoughts come into our minds, we must dash them against Christ.[34] Abba Poemen once said, "As long as the pot is on the fire, no fly nor any other animal can get near it, but as soon as it is cold, these creatures get inside. So it is for the monk; as long as he lives in spiritual activities, the enemy cannot find a means of overthrowing him."[35] If we spend our lives in peace and repentance, the Lord will be there to redeem and save us. We must simply continue to stoke our hidden fire with the fuel of passionate prayer.

Fire and light are inextricably linked. Before the electric age, the only sources of light to brighten the night throughout all of human history employed fire — torches, candles, oil lamps. Light was a scarce, precious resource. It was something to be treasured for its battles against darkness. To have a source of light with you was a matter of life or death. Thus, the weight of Christ saying that he is "the light of the world: he that followeth [him], walketh not in darkness, but shall have the light of life" (John 8:12). He who has the Lord by his side should have no fear in the face of the "principalities and powers, [the] rulers of the world of this darkness, the spirits of wickedness in the high places" (Eph 6:12). Jesus tells us that we, too, are meant to be the light of the world, and that we should shine like the sun with our clothes white as snow (Matt 5:42, 17:2). One time, "Abba Hilarion went to the mountain to Abba Anthony. Abba Anthony said to him, 'You are welcome, torch which awakens the day.' Abba Hilarion said, 'Peace to you, pillar of light, giving light to the world.'"[36] This interaction between Abba Hilarion and Abba Anthony demonstrates the close connection between external light and internal holiness. St. Seraphim of Sarov, a Russian hermit of the 19th century who emerged out of the ascetic tradition of the Northern Thebaid, once

---

[33] Ward, para. Syncletica 1.
[34] Benedict. *The Rule of St. Benedict*, (Collegeville: Liturgical Press, 1981), 3:50.
[35] Ward, para. Poemen 111.
[36] Ward, para. Hilarion 1.

startled his disciple with the physical manifestations of his transfiguration in the Holy Spirit:[37]

> Then Father Seraphim took me very firmly by the shoulders and said: 'We are both in the Spirit of God now, my son. Why don't you look at me?' I replied: 'I cannot look, Father, because your eyes are flashing like lightning. Your face has become brighter than the sun, and my eyes ache with pain.' Father Seraphim said: 'Don't be alarmed, your Godliness! Now you yourself have become as bright as I am. You are now in the fullness of the Spirit of God yourself; otherwise you would not be able to see me as I am.'[38]

The holiest monks reflected the uncreated light of the Holy Trinity in their every word, deed, and thought. In doing so, they became superior, living icons of Christ, and warmed the world around them with the gift of their presence. The ultimate calling of every Christian, not just those who are monks, is to be transformed into God's likeness by putting on the new, true man — Jesus Christ, the New Adam (Eph 4:24, 1 Cor15:45). The earliest Christian ascetics show us the way to achieve Christian perfection and give us the spiritual tools necessary to enter into union with God.

V. Conclusion

This journey into the spiritual landscape of the Desert Monastics reveals the sublime interrelations between the elemental forces of earth, water, and fire, and the quest for union with God in the lives of the earliest desert dwellers. These first Christian ascetics, through their austere and contemplative existence, exhibited a symbiotic relationship with these elements, each serving as a conduit to deeper spiritual truths. Earth, encountered in their rigorous manual labor and the simplicity of their monastic environment, emerged as a teacher of humility and self-discipline. Through tasks as prosaic as the plaiting of reeds, the monks engaged in a form of living prayer, where physical work became a medium for stillness. Water, scarce yet life-sustaining, surfaces as a symbol of God's unremitting providence and a metaphor for spiritual thirst. The monks' experiences of divine support in dire times of need serve as remarkable parables of God's nurturing

---

[37] Seraphim Rose, *The Northern Thebaid: Monastic Saints of the Russian North*, (Platina: St. Herman of Alaska Brotherhood, 2004).

[38] Valentine Zander, *St. Seraphim of Sarov*, (Yonkers: St. Vladimir's Seminary Press, 1975).

presence that emphasize the necessity of constant reliance on the Lord while striving for holiness. The slow, transformative power of water to shape landscapes over time mirrors the gradual process of increasing spiritual perfection, where persistence and faith carve out the path of sanctification. Fire, through its dynamic and metamorphic nature, encapsulates the fervor and intensity of the monastic pursuit of God. In its flames, the monks saw a reflection of the Holy Spirit's work within them, purifying and refining their souls damaged by sin. The dual functions of fire — both as a force for inner transformation and a source of illuminating, uncreated light — captures the monk's role as both a recipient and bearer of the gift of God's transfiguring grace.

The Desert Monastics' profound reverence for nature challenges contemporary Christians to re-envision our relationship with the biosphere. Their lives invite us to view the natural world not as a mere resource to be exploited, but as a sacred space that mirrors and facilitates our deeper contemplative union with God. Their examples urge us to seek harmony with Creation as we pursue Christian perfection. The intense connection the monks had with earth, water, and fire offers us a compelling, holistic model for embodied spiritual practice and an intuitive, orthodox understanding of our place within the grand tapestry of God's magnificent Creation.

9

Tom Bombadil, Bonaventure, and the Theology of Creation: On the Seven Pillars of Wisdom

Lance Gracy

What is it about Tom Bombadil, his house, and the people thereof, that prompts serious consideration on the theology of creation?[1] Tom Bombadil is Master of the Forest—of the trees, and badgers, and hills, brambles, and the like; but we could just as well look to other fantasy characters in *The Lord of the Rings* to make sense of Tolkien's perspective on the theology of creation—characters like Radagast the Brown, who's one of the "Maia of Yavanna" (Goldberry). Or perhaps we care little for fantasy and want to look only to real-life figures, like St. Francis of Assisi. In any case, I would like to draw out insights from Tolkien's work because insofar as the notion of "mastery of nature" implies "stewardship of creation," I reckon Tom makes for an excellent, albeit fantastical, paragon for thinking through creation theology. For another reason, Tolkien's catholicity is informative. Tolkien, the meticulous writer that he was, leaves clues as to *why* Tom Bombadil ought to enter our consideration as an important figure for the theology of creation, and I believe his clues lead us straightaway to the wisdom of God and creation. These clues, discerned by way of the diorama of mythopoetic lore and dialogue and assisted by anagogical themes in Tolkien's legendarium, have led me to a source beyond the text—namely, to St. Bonaventure's *Collations on the Seven Gifts of the Holy Spirit* where he discusses the seven pillars of wisdom: i.e., chastity, innocence of mind, moderation in speech, docility in affect, generosity in action, maturity of judgment, and simplicity of intention. According to Bonaventure, the house of wisdom has seven pillars, each a gift (*gratia*) of wisdom and each a

---

[1] Quick disclaimer: although I'm an avid reader of Tolkien's work, I'm no expert on his lore and legendarium so this article should not be read in that spirit. However, if readers want a deeper exploration of Tom Bombadil, I would encourage them to read Eugene Hargrove's insightful essay, a copy of which can be found here:
www.philosophy.unt.edu/~hargrove/bombadil.html.

certain step to perfect wisdom. What I will do in this article, therefore, is provide an overview of the seven pillars of wisdom. I will then relate these pillars to "the house of Tom Bombadil." Lastly, I will offer a reflection on the relevance of Bonaventure's pillars of wisdom, as they stand in view of our chosen literary model, to the theology of creation.

The First Pillar: Chastity of Body

Chastity is the first pillar of wisdom and with it is humility. Referring to an account of St. Gregory of Nazianzus while a student in Athens, Bonaventure identifies Wisdom with two maidens: humility and chastity or purity. At its root, humility is living in accord with a metaphysical truth, which for Bonaventure is a recognition of all things produced from nothing, of the nothingness of oneself and of others, and of the sublimity of the First Principle.[2] According to the *Catechism of the Catholic Church*, chastity means "the successful integration of sexuality within the person and thus the inner unity of man in his bodily and spiritual being."[3] The chaste person maintains the integrity of the vital powers, and doing so implies self-mastery of mind, body, and speech. Humility marks the beginning of chastity, and chastity marks an end to the process of humility. Together they constitute the first pillar of divine Wisdom.

A body subjected to sin is unchaste, and in an unchaste body wisdom cannot dwell, as Wisdom (1:4; 7:25; and elsewhere) states. Bonaventure draws out the rather poignant example of King Solomon, who, despite having been "filled with wisdom like a river," eventually "came to apostasy, and even to the worship of idols."[4] According to Bonaventure, it was "by a very exalted dispensation of divine counsel" that God permitted Solomon to fall: it was so that "he might teach all men to avoid women."[5] Although the wise can fall, the counsel of Wisdom is to be preferred to all things, even kingdoms and thrones (cf. Wis 7:8; 8:2, 10, 12). The counsel of Wisdom is manifold, but, generally, through it we are "elevated to choose what is permitted, appropriate, and expedient according to the norm of good will."[6] The

---

[2] Cf. Bonaventure, *Perf. Ev.,* q. 1, a.1.

[3] *CCC*, no. 2337.

[4] *Collationes de septem donis Spiritus sancti*, 9.10.

[5] Ibid., *loc. cit.*

[6] Ibid., 7.7.

judgments thereof are firmer in the heart than those of gold and silver, which "make one's feet stand secure" (cf. Sir 40:25). For Bonaventure, Sacred Scripture is symbolized by gold; the science of philosophy, by silver. "Through these sciences," says Bonaventure, "the feet are made secure, because the heart is made firm through theological and philosophical teachings." And yet, as Bonaventure adds: "Counsel makes it even more firm."[7]

There is a worthy digression we can make at this point to the cardinal virtues which descend to the soul by the four exemplary lights: From *the height of purity* is impressed the sincerity of temperance; from *the beauty of clarity* is impressed the serenity of prudence; from *the fortitude of power* is impressed the stability of perseverance; and from *the rectitude of diffusion* is impressed the sweetness of justice.[8] The first modifies, the second rectifies, the third stabilizes, and the fourth orders. For now, let us consider temperance and prudence in the context of the *influence* of the cardinal virtues according to Bonaventure's metaphorical descriptions.

Bonaventure relates the influences of the cardinal virtues in a metaphorical manner to the four elemental properties: as for temperance, the dryness and adornment of the earth; as for prudence, the transparency of water; as for fortitude, the vigor of fire; and as for justice, the softness of the air.[9] It seems clear from Tolkien's descriptions of Goldberry that her chastity is associated most with temperance and prudence, as her image is associated most with the earth, the flowers, and the river. Indeed, it was far down the Withywindle, by a pool, where Tom found the River-daughter, "sitting in the rushes." Her singing was sweet, "and her heart was beating." She is adorned in silver and gold, which is indicative of the counsel of philosophy and Scripture. She represents one filled with wisdom "like a river." Borne of the pools of the Withywindle, she is the "River-daughter" and "River-maiden." These appellations are allusions to St. Francis's *Laudes Creaturarum*, wherein "Sister Water"—which for Bonaventure is metaphorical name for the *beauty of clarity* impressing the *serenity of prudence*—is described as "very useful, and humble, and precious, and pure (*multo utile et humile et pretiosa et casta*)."

---

[7] Ibid., *loc. cit.*

[8] Bonaventure, *Collationes in Hexaëmeron*, 6.10.

[9] Ibid., 6.21.

Goldberry's purity or chastity is enhanced by the river lilies associated with her. Tom loves to pick lilies for Goldberry and he describes her as having "flowers in her girdle." When the hobbits first meet Goldberry, they describe her as "an elf-queen clad in living flowers" and they notice, about her feet, "in wide vessels of green and brown earthenware," white water-lilies floating, "so that she seemed to be enthroned in the midst of a pool." Traditionally, the lily is a symbol of purity and chastity. In Goldberry's case, lilies become for her a vision of her purity in that they speak to her adornment by temperance. The metaphorical name of "Sister Mother Earth"—who "sustains an s governs us and who produces various fruit with colored flowers and herbs"—is *the height of purity* impressing *sincerity of temperance.* These definite allusions to Goldberry, which relate quite directly to Bonaventure's metaphorical descriptions of temperance and prudence, speak to what I would call "the counsel of chastity." Chastity is evidently pure, sincerely serene, and dearly beloved.

The imagery of Tom and Goldberry is profoundly consonant with a Christian view of the New Creation. The origins of Tom's and Goldberry's love are as if that of holy Joseph finding his chaste spouse, Mary, abreast holy waters, singing a new song of Creation for the joy belonging to her as the New Eve and as the New Ark of the Covenant, who housed the ineffable mystery of the Redeemer of Creation inside of her. Unlike miscreants lusting for the goddess Artemis bathing in the forest, the holy man does not devour the chaste woman with his eyes; rather, the chaste woman devours any trace of impurity with her gaze, co-fixed by the eternal gaze of the Truth, thus instilling a new desire in the holy man—a desire to honor the precious, chaste daughter of the River of Eternal Life and to work most diligently amid the timbers and things of the Old, and New, Forest— the work entrusted uniquely to him. As Hargrove has argued, Tom and Goldberry may in fact be Aulë and Yavanna respectively, the Ainur embodied as Vala, offspring of Ilúvatar's thought not "gods" *per se,* but emissaries and regents of Ilúvatar, to serve as elders and guides for the Children of Ilúvatar (i.e., Elves and Men). Hence the Valar can say, with the Wise: "My delight is to be with the children of men and women" (8:31). The identity of Tom and Goldberry makes sense, given not only that most of the Valar are married, but also because the descriptions of Aulë and Yavanna fit neatly with those of Tom and

Goldberry.[10] I suspect as well that perhaps Tolkien had St. Francis and St. Clare in mind with his descriptions.

The Second Pillar: Innocence of Mind

If chastity is the guardian of wisdom, the second pillar, innocence of mind, is the warden of chastity. Innocence of mind pertains to the political virtue of justice, which is concerned perhaps most of all with peaceable and patient order of things as exercised through humility. As Bonaventure says: "It pertains to political justice to safeguard for each one what is one's own, and from justice come innocence, friendship, piety, religion (*religio*), affect (*affectus*), and humanity."[11] Quoting Augustine's *De Civitate Dei*—"The peace of all things is the tranquility of order"—Bonaventure holds that war and infighting, which leads to the destruction of (inner) peace, is caused by social disruption of the bonds of order, which includes the social bonds of (a) humbly submitting oneself to one's superior, (b) being impartial with one's equals, and (c) being discretely superior to one's subjects.[12] The balm for navigating social conflicts—which can, if left unattended, lead to war, infighting, and the like—is patience. As a disposition and sign of behavior that is governed by the meekness of wisdom, patience is indeed a virtue; but more so it is an indispensable part of humility, the virtues of the innocence of mind, and of life lived with a "good conscience" (cf. 1 Tim 1:19). But how is it that patience is not possessed? It is as what Bonaventure says about humility in his *Collationes in Hexaëmeron*: "The fire is not guarded in the midst of the ashes, but our lamp is exposed to every wind, and the lamp is quickly extinguished."[13] To guard peace and patience is to guard the fire of devotion. So then, innocence of mind requires the stabilizing

---

[10] Aulë is one of the Aratar, smith, master of crafts, and spouse of Yavanna. Tom Bombadil—who has many names; "Bombadil" is Bucklandish in origin and signifies, at the very least, the relation Tom has with the hobbits and, indirectly, to the fate of the Ring—demonstrates arcane knowledge of the weapons found in the Barrow-Downs—relics of the Men of Westernesse, of Númenor—and this makes him a likely candidate; yet the descriptions of Yavanna seems even more fitting. Yavanna is giver of fruits, one of the Valier, numbered among the Aratar. As queen of the Earth, her patronage is associated more with plants and vegetation than with animals.

[11] *Hex.*, 6.29.

[12] *Collationes de septem donis Spiritus sancti*, 9.11.

[13] *Hex.*, 1.24.

influence of fortitude and the rectifying moral power of justice.

The house of Under Hill is a chapel of light, nature, and hope; a most peaceful refuge from the corruption of the Old Forest, the dread of the Barrow wights, and the shadows of Melkor and his servants. When Frodo becomes overly curious about one of the creatures of the Old Forest, Old Man Willow, and forgets to pay heed to Tom's words, Merry and Pippin tell him to wait until morning to ask. This can be seen as an instance of impartiality among equals, which serves the purpose of attaining innocence and peace of mind. After Merry and Pippin correct Frodo, Tom says: "Sleep till the morning-light, rest on the pillow! Heed no nightly noise! Fear no grey willow!" Throughout the night, Frodo hears the creaks and cracks of nature outside the house. These "nightly noises" are like the clamoring of the world, potential causes of unrest. It is only upon Frodo hearing again the words, "Fear nothing! Have peace until morning! Heed no nightly noises!" that he falls back to sleep. As we can see then, innocence of mind—with its accompanying powers of fortitude and justice—speaks to discerning God's voice amid the tumultuousness of a fallen creation. Think here of the Prophet Elijah.

After taking refuge in the cleft of the Rock at Mt. Horeb, and after fleeing the prophets of Baal seeking to kill him, he is called out of the cave by God, who will soon pass by. Forces of nature come; only, God was not in the wind (represented as the "clamor of political life" rather than the "softness of the air"), nor in the earthquake (represented as the *instability* of the earth rather than the stability), nor in the fire (represented as over-zealousness rather than pure vigor). The sheer silence that follows the forces of nature prompts Elijah to come closer. There, in the stillness, God speaks to Elijah, saying: "Go, return on your way to the wilderness of Damascus, when you arrive, you shall anoint Hazael as king over Aram" (2 Kgs 9:15). While Frodo will not directly anoint a king, it is still not difficult to see how Frodo's need for clear instruction (from Gandalf, from Tom, and others) is importantly related to another need: to have refuge of mind from the Black Riders who seek to take his life—to have, like Elijah, refreshment and respite from the noises, injustices, and extremities of the world.

Fair Goldberry, too, whose song "began merrily in the hills and fell softly down into silence," is a cause of respite for the hobbits' troubles, for by these songs the hobbits see in their minds "pools and waters wider than any they had known, and looking into them they saw the sky below them and the stars like jewels in the depths." (Interestingly, Bonaventure associates the unity of cardinal and theological virtues with such deep, consoling constellations). To be in the innocence of mind and its peaceableness permits the perfected visions of purity, beauty, power, and goodness to enter the mind.

The Third Pillar: Moderation of Speech

Moderation of speech is of utmost importance, for "Death and life are in the power of the tongue" (Prov 18:21). Furthermore, it is important because by speech the wisdom of God's creation is expressed. Moderation of speech consists in knowing when and when not to speak; keeping silence; "weighing words" as if measuring and balancing them (Sir 28:29); to be very careful to avoid excessive talking, and so forth. As Sirach states: "A wise man will be silent till the right time comes, but a babbler and a fool will not pay attention to the time" (20:7). Bonaventure quotes Cato: "I consider the first of the virtues to curb the tongue."[14] For Bonaventure, moderation of speech is so important to wisdom because, on one hand, if Eve had kept silent, the devil would have had no occasion to tempt her further, and because, on the other hand, "the sins of the tongue are so great that the world would have enough to do to make satisfaction for them alone if God were to rise in judgment against them."[15] It is a remarkable thing, from Bonaventure's vantage, to sit at a table to refresh oneself spiritually, only to then talk about temporal affairs and detractions, which poison all at the table.[16] In this way, talk of temporal affairs can detract from the natural and spiritual betterment of creatures. At the table of Tom Bombadil, two modes of speech are prevalent: silent attention to business, or mirth, laughter, and singing—the latter of which seemed "easier and more natural than talking" to the hobbits. These two modes are, I believe, well-suited to the third pillar of wisdom, and are prevalent only with someone like Tom, who stays mindful of the right time for speaking. As he says in response to Frodo's questioning about Willow-Man: "Now is the time for resting. Some things are ill to hear when the world's in shadow."

---

[14] *Collationes de septem donis Spiritus sancti*, 9.12.

[15] Ibid., *loc. cit.*

[16] Ibid., *loc. cit.*

Of course, none of this should be taken to mean that there's never an appropriate time for long tales of much speaking. Indeed, Tom tells the hobbits many remarkable tales—tales that "laid bare the hearts" of creatures, which were "often dark and strange," and which leapt across streams, waterfalls, pebbles and worn rocks, flowers and wet crannies. But all these marvelous tales were told on "a good day for long tales, for questions and for answers."

The Fourth Pillar: Docility in Affect

Given the difficulty of persuading someone toward moderation of speech, it is fitting that the next pillar of wisdom, docility in affect, acts as its support. As Bonaventure says, "Docility brings about a high regard for good things, and it makes one love them and consent to them."[17] Docility is a kindly spirit of the affects persuading one by good speech. Thus, docility is tied to good speech. Kind words, especially those that reprove the wise, adorn one like a beautiful earring or like a pearl about the face (Prov 25:12). The kind words of docility are not "nice" words, though. They are, rather, sincere words devoid of malintent. To be kind is to give knowing one will use what is given well. Bonaventure thinks the whole world is seated in wickedness (cf. 1 Jn 5:19) because people ignore such kindness and love only their own private good, by which he means people give of themselves to others knowing that the other will use what is given wrongly.[18] When those with an ear to wisdom hear kind words, they correct themselves, are adorned, and glad. The arrogant do no such thing.

Goldberry's words to the hobbits speak to *Qoheleth* (Ecclesiastes) 10:12: "Words in the mouth of a wise person are grace." The hobbits enjoyed observing Goldberry, as "the slender grace of her movement filled them with quiet delight." While Goldberry's words and behavior are kindly, they are perhaps not the best example of the form of kindness that reproves the wise. For that, it is appropriate to recall the words of the High Elves to Frodo as the hobbits were passing through the Eastfarthing. After Frodo tells the High Elves that he would welcome their company, the Elves respond: "But we have no need of other company, and hobbits are so dull." Rather than become

---

[17] Ibid., 9.13.

[18] Cf. *Hex.*, 5.9.

indignant at this, the hobbits explain their situation, and once the Elves entreat their journey, Frodo thanks them in the Ancient Tongue: "*Elen sila lúmenn omentielvo*, a star shines on the hour of our meeting." The Elves are pleased with this, and when Frodo first meets Goldberry, he praises her with a beautiful quatrain heard previously, to which Goldberry laughs: "I had not heard that folk of the Shire were so sweet-tongued. But I see you are an elf-friend; the light in your eyes and the ring in your voice tells it." The reward of the wise, who love those who reprove them, is the docility of affect—in this case, the greater compliment borne from the prior stings of friends.

The relation of good and kind speech to the theology of creation becomes particularly evident in Goldberry's response to Frodo when he asks her whether the land (i.e., the Forest) belongs to Tom. "No indeed!" answers Goldberry. "That would indeed be a burden." Goldberry corrects Frodo here. Living things belong to themselves. Tom is master and has no fear of them and is not caught by them. But the living things do not belong to him. Living things belong to themselves and can do so only inasmuch as they belong to God, who made them for themselves and for himself.

The Fifth Pillar: Generosity of Action

Generosity of action is related to docility in affect; however, it is more concerned with the effects of mercy rather than the affect of good speech. Bonaventure quotes from Proverbs: "She has opened her hand to the needy and she extends her palms to the poor. She has opened her mouth to wisdom, and the law of mercy is on her tongue. From the fruit of her hands she gives to the needy" (cf. Prov 31:20, 26, 16). The wisdom of generosity of action pertains to munificence, right administration, and fecundity—with mercy as its chief friend. Its enemy is avarice.

As Lavanna, the "giver of fruits," Goldberry is hospitable. Indeed, Tom and Goldberry treat the hobbits as lavishly as one might expect:

> Tom opened the door, and they followed him down a short passage and round a sharp turn. They came to a low room with a sloping roof (a penthouse, it seemed, built on to the north end of the house)…There were four deep mattresses, each piled with white blankets, laid on the floor along one side. Against the opposite wall was a long bench laden with wide earthenware basins, and beside it stood brown ewers filled with water, some cold, some steaming hot. There were soft green slippers set

ready beside each bed.

Tom gives a clue as to his thoughts on generosity. After second supper, Tom tells the hobbits a variety of tales. One such tale is about the Barrow-downs, of kings and queens of old fighting for their little kingdoms—where the "young Sun shone like fire on the red metal of their new and greedy swords." The greed of these kings and queens is signified by their fate—as gauntly wights roaming the mounds of the Barrow-downs, they tend to the gold "piled on the biers of dead kings and queens." If the living lay to heart the cries of the mournful (Ecc 7:2), the perspicacious lay to heart the reason thereof. In other words, the living, if they are wise, ought to heed the wisdom of the dead. Better to go to the house of giving than to go to the tomb of the greedy. And better to be a wise servant standing against an unwise king than to be an unwise king standing against a wise servant.[19]

The Sixth Pillar: Mature Judgment

As Psalm 36:60 reads: "The mouth of the just one will meditate wisdom, and his tongue will speak judgment." The one who has maturity of judgment does not judge rashly, and he judges all those over whom he has authority without going beyond his authority.[20] One who judges well, or has maturity of judgment, is "moved by just zeal to approve everything that is good and to disapprove of what is evil."[21] One should not judge if he is without correct zeal and clear knowledge, but if one must judge another, it would be better for him to think good of that person rather than evil, for "A person should be more inclined to excuse kindly than to accuse wrongly." Bonaventure writes that it is "the highest form of foolishness when people judge the personal faults of others and overlook themselves."[22] Citing St. Gregory, Bonaventure adds: "The more curious a mind is to pry into the affairs of others, the more foolish it is in knowing its own affairs."[23]

Tom's judgments are mature. His knowledge of creatures is clear and his zeal correct. He "knows the tune of old Willow Man." He

---

[19] Cf. *Collationes de septem donis Spiritus sancti*, 9.7.

[20] Ibid., 9.16.

[21] Ibid., *loc. cit.*

[22] Ibid., *loc. cit.*

[23] Ibid., *loc. cit.*

knows the history of Men and Elves. He seems by all appearances quite near the epitome of mature judgment. Tom doesn't venture beyond his authority, nor does he venture beyond the boundaries he has set for himself. St. Paul's words to the church at Thessalonica—"to aspire to live quietly, to mind your own affairs, and to work with your hands" so that you "may behave properly towards outsiders and be dependent on no one" (1 Thess 4:11-12)—seems well satisfied in Tom.

The Seventh Pillar: Simplicity of Intention

The seventh pillar of the house of wisdom is simplicity of intention. In a word, this is holy commonsense; a foundation of thought and action sourced above, not below. It is the certain step of the wise architect, who builds on a solid foundation that is not of the earth or world, but upon Christ, who is seated with God in heaven. Bonaventure writes:

> [I]n terms of its root, the human being is just the opposite of the tree. The tree has its root down below while the human person has its root above. And a bodily building has its foundation down below, while a spiritual edifice has its foundation above. Christ, therefore, is the foundation of this gift...he is its completion, for 'in him are hidden all the treasure of wisdom and knowledge.' In him the gift of wisdom is brought to completion.[24]

Tom Bombadil's simplicity of intention is a saying and manner seasoned in uncommon wisdom, that is all but common to the wise. It is not the "common wisdom" of the farmer. It is, rather, an uncommon wisdom of the farmer. Tom is a friend of Farmer Maggot, a hobbit-farmer of the Eastfarthing, and praises him: "There's earth under his old feet, and clay on his fingers; wisdom in his bones, and both his eyes are open." Tom is not "grounded" or rooted in the wisdom of the earth. He is, rather, beyond it. He is untrusting of the trees, whose "rooted wisdom" has now become "full of pride." If 'truth' and 'tree' derive from the same root, that root could only be from the Tree of Life—for the natural doings of the earth can be strange, dark, and corrupt. As Bonaventure states:

> Do not, therefore, be wise concerning 'things that are of the earth,' because Christ was crucified to do away with this kind of wisdom. As

---

[24] Ibid., 9.17.

Christ died to do away with and destroy vain wisdom, so he rose and ascended in order to teach true wisdom and to confirm it in our hearts…[He] taught how to desire the wisdom of God and to love the Fount of Life.[25]

As Tom Bombadil's desire is for the offspring of Ilúvatar, so Bonaventure's desire is for Christ, the only begotten Son of God and the one true teacher of men. In him, we learn true wisdom. I would even go so far as to say: in Christ, we men can be like Tom Bombadil, and women can be like Goldberry!

Being in the Wisdom of God's Creation

From humility to chastity, from peace of mind to right speech, and from docility and kindness to generosity and maturity of judgment— these "certain steps" lead us to a final step, simplicity of intention, which completes the Solomonic Throne of the Wisdom of God's Creation (cf. Prov 9:1), in which one becomes properly religious and deepens in humility and wisdom. This deepening of humility is like the deepening of a river, making the soul more deiform and transparent to others, which in turn deepens everything that relates to the affect. Going from and back, this *concentricity* of wisdom forms a habit—a *consummation of Being through the order of essential relation between God and Creation*—of continual recognition of our dependence upon the Divine Exemplar, Christ, the foundation and source of life beyond the rudiments of the world.

The house of God's Creation is built mainly by wisdom, as Bonaventure says.[26] The house of Tom Bombadil is a remarkable image of the wisdom of creation. His house is beautifully and wonderfully arranged, which further connects with Bonaventure's view that the house of wisdom is delightful, beautiful, and strong: it brings joy to our affective power and strengthens our power of action; it "makes the intellective power beautiful, the affective power delightful, and the operative power robust."[27] The house of Under Hill is itself reminiscent of a chapel of light and nature, situated on the outskirts of the Old Forest near Buckland and nestled beneath the Barrow-Downs, where the gauntly wights of the kings and queens of

---

[25] Ibid., 9.4.

[26] Ibid., 9.8.

[27] *Hex.*, 2.1.

---

old roam, and this latter detail serves as a lesson to heed divine counsel and the simplicity of intention. The house of Under Hill speaks to the purity of the wisdom of God's creation (chastity); the refuge of the wisdom of God's creation (innocence of mind and peace); the moderation of the wisdom of God's creation (speech); the affectivity of the wisdom of God's creation (docility and kindness); the bountifulness of the wisdom of God's creation (generosity of action); the mature thinking of the wisdom of God's creation (maturity of judgment); and the foundation of the wisdom of God's creation (simplicity of intention).

If you're like me, you often think about what the theology of creation *means* in terms of *the doing*. What can stewards and defenders of creation *do* amid corruption, evil, and dread? I think this is akin to asking: *How ought we live as lovers of the wisdom of God's Creation?* Is *our* vocation, we lovers of God's Creation, not very much like Tom Bombadil and Goldberry? Could it be that God is instructing us *to be* and *to do* in the house of Wisdom, and to prefer nothing else to it? And what would it mean for our manner of life to reflect such—to live as stewards of the wisdom of God's Creation?

In a climactic episode following the second supper in the house of Master Tom, we see Tom ask Frodo for the Ring. Frodo gives it to Tom unhesitatingly. Tom plays with it a bit and slips it on the end of his finger; but he doesn't disappear. The hobbits are alarmed by this, but Tom laughs, spins the Ring in the air, causing the Ring to vanish, and then when Frodo cries out for it, Tom returns it to him. When Tom returns the Ring, Frodo looks at it closely "and rather suspiciously, like one who has lent a trinket to a juggler." I cannot help but think of St. Francis here—the *jongleur de Dieu*, God's holy jester and fool. I reflected more deeply about of Tom's imperviousness to the power of the Ring. What I think it shows is that a wise and peaceful heart, aided by some mysterious source and, in part, by its "odd caperings," can properly spurn the enticements and allurements of the world. Like a fiery seraphic sword, Tom is a guardian, driving the hobbits away from the tree of life (*flammeum gladium atque versatilem ad custodiendam viam ligni vitae*) through his very manner of life. Certainly, the Ring has the power of immortality, but not the power of immortality of the lowly and humble. As guardian and steward, Tom Bombadil illustrates something of a pilgrim of metaphysical reflection and apt imitation of Christ as efficient restorer and truth of Creation. His book is an internal book of creation inscribed in the soul and fading into the external. More than a defender of creation, he is a steward. More than a steward, he is a wise guardian of sacred wisdom. Perhaps, then, Tolkien's work recalls forgotten distinctions—distinctions concerning *the steward, the guardian, the defender* and the ways in which these relate to a question of *nature versus creation.* If we were to question further, we could ask: How do these archetypes, if we may call them that, relate to a social-political philosophy pertinent to the theology of creation? It seems for the creation theologian, the doing is in the being.

But we have work to do, and "Goldberry is waiting."

God Works All Things for Good: The Role of the Devil in Divine Providence and the Permission of Evil

Gideon Lazar

"We know that in everything God works for good" (Rom 8:28).[1] In this quote, St. Paul answers an age-old question: if God is all-powerful and all-good, why does evil exist? Two basic answers to this question existed in the ancient world: monism (the denial that God is all-good, as He must contain evil in Himself) and dualism (the denial that God is all-powerful, as He must have an equally powerful foe).[2] Paul however rejects this false dichotomy: God permits evil for the sake of good. While here Paul says that God does this "with those who love Him," over the following chapters Paul goes on to prove that God uses even the actions of the wicked for the sake of good.

While Paul does not apply this principle to the Devil explicitly, the same principle still undoubtedly applies. While God does not cause the Devil to commit any evil acts, He permits such acts so that He can providentially order them to the common good of the universe.

In order to understand this, we will first need to cover the nature of evil. For this we will look at the writings of Dionysius.[3] Dionysius provides one of the most extensive Patristic accounts of the nature of evil and its relationship to providence. Dionysius only briefly treats the role of the Devil, so we will the look at the Book of Job where the role of the Devil plays in divine providence plays a central role to the larger message of the book. Finally, we will consider what this greater

---

[1] Biblical translations taken from the Revised Standard Version, Catholic Edition.

[2] For a history of these positions in the ancient world, see Jeffery Burton Russell, *The Devil: Perceptions of Evil from Antiquity to Primitive Christianity*, (Ithaca: Cornell University Press, 1977); *Satan: The Early Christian Tradition*, (Ithaca: Cornell University Press, 1981).

[3] The writings of Dionysius were for a long time in both East and West taken to be the writings of the companion of St. Paul, St. Dionysius the Areopagite. However, in the fifteenth century, significant evidence against the authenticity of these works began to mount. Thus, he is frequently referred to today as "Ps. Dionysius." I have opted in this essay to simply adopt the convention of referring to the author of these works as "Dionysius" as this is the name he refers to himself by.

good is that God permits evil for.

I. Providence and the Nature of Evil

Dionysius provides one of the most detailed Patristic accounts of the nature (or really lack-thereof) of evil in *On Divine Names*. In this work, Dionysius seeks to understand how God can be given any name at all given that He is infinitely beyond all things. Drawing on Neoplatonism, Dionysius reasons that since God is the source of all things, He must somehow pre-contain all things as the cause of these effects.

One of the names Dionysius uses to refer to God's presence and causality in the world is "providence."[4] For Dionysius, God is not the source of things in the sense of a deistic God. Rather, God is the source of things both in their origin and sustenance, as God is beyond the differences of time that occur within creation itself. God produces all things in an eternal now. Creation and providence are really distinct to us, but they are one and the same action in God. Thus, God is named not merely from His effects at the moment of creation, but from his effects in His providential guidance of things. Dionysius explains that,

> since, as sustaining source of goodness, by the very fact of Its being, It is cause of all things that be, from all created things must we celebrate the benevolent Providence of the Godhead; for all things are both around It and for It, and It is before all things, and all things in It consist, and by Its being is the production and sustenance of the whole, and all things aspire to It.[5]

Dionysius thus seems much more in the "monist" category than the "dualist" category. Nonetheless, unlike many ancient pagan monists, Dionysius refuses to say that God is not all-good. He repeatedly refers to God as good and insists that God is "guiltless of things evil."[6] This seems to pose a problem. In fact, Dionysius himself is well aware of this problem. As he himself asks, "How, in short, are there evils when there is a Providence?"[7]

Nonetheless, Dionysius does think this question can be answered. He first starts by considering some basic metaphysical principles.

---

[4] Eric D. Perl, *Theophany: The Neoplatonic Philosophy of Dionysius the Areopagite*, (Albany: State University of New York Press, 2007), 29.
[5] Dionysius the Areopagite, *The Divine Names*, in *The Works of Dionysius the Areopagite*, vol. 1, trans. John Parker, (London: James Parker and Co., 1897), I.5.
[6] Dionysius, IV.35.
[7] Dionysius, IV.33.

> The Evil, *qua* evil, is not, neither as an actual thing nor as in things existing… For neither is the Evil an actual thing existing unmixed with the Good. And, if no single thing is without participation in the Good, but the lack of the Good is an evil, and no existing thing is deprived absolutely of the Good.[8]

Dionysius follows the Platonic and Aristotelian traditions in denying an equal ontological footing to good and evil. Goodness is a property of being. While being can exist in distinct modes, such as act and potency, insofar as any of these are being, they are good. Good and evil are thus not modes of being. Rather, evil is some privation of goodness. It would almost seem then that evil cannot have existence. However, Dionysius allows that being exists "as an accident."[9] That is, being exists not in itself, but by inhering in another, and that other it inheres in must itself be good in order to exist.

It is on this basis that Dionysius can give a key metaphysical insight. Since God is the source of all being, "the Divine Providence is in all existing things, and no single thing is without Providence."[10] Thus, while God's providence cannot itself be the cause of the evil, the good thing the evil inheres in is still itself subject to providence. Hence, "Providence, as befits Its goodness, uses even evils which happen for the benefit, either individual or general, of themselves or others, and suitably provides for each being."[11] God uses the good substance in which the accident of evil inheres, and hence uses the evil without Himself being its cause.

It might be objected at this point that evil cannot ever originate though, since if the substances God creates are all good, how can every of those substances give rise to an evil, even accidentally. It would seem that the act of bringing about the evil must itself be beyond providence, something Dionysius already denied. However, Dionysius turns the argument on its head.

> As Providence is conservative of the nature of each, it provides for the free, as free; and for the whole, and individuals, according to the wants of all and each, as far as the nature of those provided for admits the providential benefits of its universal and manifold Providence, distributed proportionably to each.[12]

---

8 Dionysius, IV.33.
9 Dionysius, I.32.
10 Dionysius, IV.33.
11 Dionysius, IV.33.
12 Dionysius, IV.33.

God is able to bring about agents that are naturally free. That these creatures be free is part of providence. Thus, the creatures can freely choose to bring about evil. Nonetheless, the evil they bring about will only be accidental, and hence God will be able to use that evil to bring about good, nonetheless.

Dionysius applies this reasoning not only to human evil, but also to angelic evil.

> As for the demons, what they are is both from the Good, and good. But their evil is from the declension from their own proper goods, and a change----the weakness, as regards their identity and condition, of the angelic perfection befitting them. And they aspire to the Good, in so far as they aspire to be and to live and to think. And in so far as they do not aspire to the Good, they aspire to the non-existent; and this is not aspiration, but a missing of the true aspiration.[13]

The demons, insofar as they exist, are still good. In another work, *The Celestial Hierarchies*, Dionysius explicates all the various glories of the different ranks of angels. The demons were called to share in these glories. Nonetheless, they willingly rejected them.

For Dionysius then, the Devil is not some great malevolent power challenging God in a dualistic sense. Rather, the Devil is a pathetic weakling who rejected his own good, and in the process only further serves God anyways.

While Dionysius provides a profound metaphysical account of the relationship between providence and evil, his logic comes for the most part from Neoplatonism. As a result, his views are sometimes dismissed as unbiblical. Martin Luther for example dismissed his writings as "more Platonist than Christian."[14] Is this an accurate assessment? For this, we will have to apply his analysis to the Book of Job.

II. The Role of the Devil in the Book of Job

According to St. Thomas Aquinas, the primary theme of the book of Job is "to show that human affairs are ruled by divine providence using probable arguments."[15] Rudi te Velde has pointed out that St.

---

[13] Dionysius, IV.34.

[14] Cited in Perl, 2. Translation my own.

[15] Thomas Aquinas, *Commentary on the Book of Job*, trans. Brian Thomas Beckett Mullady, (Steubenville, Emmaus Academic, 2016), pro.3.

Thomas authored his commentary on Job around the same time as he authored the *Summa contra Gentiles*, the entire third book of which is dedicated to the metaphysics of divine providence.[16] In the *contra Gentiles*, Thomas offers a metaphysical account of providence very similar to, and inspired by, Dionysius. While, as te Velde demonstrates, Thomas applies those same principles to the Book of Job, the difference given by Thomas is that Job uses "probable arguments." Job gives us a particular example of these philosophical principles and so demonstrates to us that providence is not some abstract philosophical idea, but something very pertinent to how the universe actually functions.

Job is especially important for understanding the role of the Devil, for this is one of the few books of scripture he appears in. He appears however only in the first two chapters of the book. Here is given the Hebrew title of *Satan*, meaning adversary.[17] The role of the Devil in the cosmos is to go about serving as an adversary to mankind.

Satan is said to come into the presence of God (Job 1:6). This is quite shocking given that Satan is usually portrayed as cast out of heaven. However, St. Thomas says that this passage shows how

> it is fitting not only for the good angels, but also the wicked ones and even men to assist in the presence of God, because whatever is done by them is subject to the divine gaze and examination.[18]

Satan, even in his attempt to accuse man before God, is still serving God's purposes within divine providence. Thus, Satan is a servant of God precisely in fulfilling the role of adversary.

When great calamities befall Job, Job rightly recognizes that it is the work of divine providence. "Naked I came from my mother's womb, and naked shall I return; the Lord gave, and the Lord has taken away; blessed be the name of the Lord" (Job 1:21). He rightly recognizes that God is provident over all things. Nonetheless, Job's friends visit him and try to convince him that there must be fault on the part of Job.

---

[16] Rudi te Velde, "Divine Providence and Man's Place in the Order of the Good," in *Reading Job with St. Thomas Aquinas*, eds. Matthew Levering, Piotr Roszak, and Jörgen Vijgen, (Washington, D.C.: The Catholic University of America Press, 2020), 127-142.

[17] Blue Letter Bible, "H7854 – śāṭān – Strong's Hebrew Lexicon," accessed July 12, 2024, https://www.blueletterbible.org/lexicon/h7854.

[18] Aquinas, C1.L2.n12.

Much of the rest of the book is dedicated to an extensive dialogue between Job and his friends as they attempt to determine why this is happening. At the end of the book, God himself appears to Job to give him the answer. Many have felt troubled at the ending of Job, as God does not seem to mention the role of Satan at the beginning of the book. Instead, God goes on about all the complexities of the cosmos and asks Job whether he has had to run any of these things. In all these things, God demonstrates to Job the complexity of divine providence. We cannot have an easy answer to why bad things happen to good people. If we had a comprehensive knowledge of the whole universe and all of history, the answer would become obvious, but we are not in that place.

While Satan is not explicitly named in these chapters, this does not mean he is excluded from them. At the end of his speech, God names two great beasts He has made, Behemoth and Leviathan. The precise identity of these beings is subject to dispute. St. Ephrem the Syrian considered them to be land and sea dragons.[19] St. Thomas Aquinas considered them to be the elephant and the whale.[20] Still others have suggested that these are dinosaurs,[21] or that these are purely mythical beasts.[22] Regardless of what they actually are, St. Thomas points out that,

> the properties of these animals are described as a metaphor of something else. This is clear because, after he has described the characteristics pertaining to this figure, He explains their meaning here. After he has described the properties of the Behemoth, that is, the elephant, he explains the truth, saying, "he is the principle of the ways of God." When he has explained the properties of the Leviathan, that is, the whale, he says, "he is the king over all the sons of pride" (Job 41:25). The disputation of Job is finished, fittingly enough, with a description of the devil, who is his adversary, because Satan was the cause of all his suffering in the first place (Job 1:12). So, because the friends of Job strove to refer the cause of the adversities of Job to Job himself, and thought he was punished because of his sins, the Lord, after he contradicted Job about the lack of order in his speech, makes the final

---

[19] Ephrem the Syrian, *Commentary on Job*, 40:15, cited in *Job*, eds. Marco Conti and Manlio Simonetti, *Ancient Christian Commentary on Scripture: Old Testament*, vol. 6, (Downers Grove: InterVarsity Press, 2006), eBook.

[20] Aquinas, C40.L2.n536.

[21] James B. Jordan, *Through New Eyes: Developing a Biblical View of the World*, (Brentwood: Wolgemuth & Hyatt, Publishers, Inc., 1988), 99.

[22] Robert S. Fyall, *Now My Eyes Have Seen You: Images of Creation and Evil in the Book of Job*, (Downers Grove: IVP Academic, 2002), 126-129.

determination of the argument and treats the evil of Satan, which was the beginning of the adversity of Job, and is the beginning of human damnation.

God ends his speech with two allegories of Satan to demonstrate, without even naming him, that the devil too is within the control of divine providence.[23]

Although these creatures are too fierce to be controlled by man, nonetheless they are still within the scope of divine providence as well. Behemoth is still one of "the works of God" and Leviathan is those which is "under the whole heaven" and thus ruled by God (Job 40:19, 41:11). God rules even Satan and directs all his evil acts towards the end of divine providence.

Nonetheless, God does end on the final note that Leviathan "is king over all the sons of pride" (Job 41:34). While God works the Devil's evil acts towards a good end, we still have the free will to act pridefully and thus fall under the dominion of the Devil. While God will work all things for the common good of the universe, He will not work things in a way that is personally good for Satan. Satan is still fully culpable for his actions, since, as Dionysius proved, part of God's providence is to allow for free will. If we choose to act sinfully, we too could be one of those instruments that God uses towards a greater good despite our evil. Not the greater good of us personally, but the common good of the whole universe.

III. The Greatest Good

We have thus demonstrated that even the evil deeds of the Devil are under the control of divine providence. God does indeed work all things for good. This leaves open the question though of what this good is. While Dionysius does not mention providence in the last chapter of *Divine Names*, Harry Marsh suggests that Dionysius implies that "the goal of the providential governance of the universe is the perfection and unity of all things."[24] Since Dionysius reasons

---

[23] Robert Fyall agrees that Leviathan is a symbol of Satan but thinks that Behemoth is a symbol of the Canaanite god Mot. Fyall, 130-137. This would not pose any issue for the argument in this paper, as the "the gods of the nations are demons" (Ps 95:5 LXX). Hence God would instead be starting with a lesser demon before dealing with the chief one who accused Job in the beginning of the book.

[24] Harry C. Marsh, "Cosmic Structure and the Knowledge of God: Thomas Aquinas'

only at a philosophical level about providence, his answer, while good, only gets to a philosophical conclusion. What precisely is that perfection and unity that God is working all things towards?

Satan says that Job only continues to praise God because God has not taken his life.

> Skin for skin! All that a man has he will give for his life. But put forth thy hand now, and touch his bone and his flesh, and he will curse thee to thy face (Job 2:4-5).

While God forbids Satan from killing Job, Job eventually concludes that even if his life were taken, he would still praise God:

> For I know that my Redeemer lives, and at last he will stand upon the earth; and after my skin has been thus destroyed, then from my flesh I shall see God, whom I shall see on my side, and my eyes shall behold, and not another. My heart faints within me! (Job 19:25-27)

Job realizes here that this life is not as significant as the age to come.[25]

Job does not merely speak here of the age to come. He says that he will see God "from the flesh." Thus, God must at this time be perceptible to the eyes. Job thus gives a prophecy of the incarnation!

It is here that we have the answer to the great question of why God permits evil. The infinite goodness which God pours forth on the cross in redeeming us from sin outweighs any evil which could ever exist! For the infinite goodness of God necessarily surpasses any sins proper to finite creatures.

In librum Beatii Dionysii de Divinis Nominibus Expositio," PhD dissertation, Vanderbilt University, 1994, 186.

[25] This is the traditional interpretation of the passage. See for example Aquinas, C19.L2; Ephrem the Syrian, 19:25; John Chrysostom, *Commentary on Job*, 19:25-26, in *Job*, eds. Marco Conti and Manlio Simonetti. This interpretation has received significant criticism in modern biblical criticism on the grounds that later Christian theology would not have been Job's concern. However, Fyall argues convincingly that this actually fits well within the context. Job is concerned about whether God is his adversary or his vindicator, and here he leans towards the latter rather than the former. Fyall, 44-52.